Weapons
OF THE
Lewis & Clark Expedition

Weapons

OF THE

Lewis & Clark Expedition

By Jim Garry

THE ARTHUR H. CLARK COMPANY

An imprint of the University of Oklahoma Press

Norman, Oklahoma

2012

ALSO BY JIM GARRY

This Ol' Drought Ain't Broke Us Yet (But We're All Bent Pretty Bad): Stories of the American West (New York, 1992)

The First Liar Never Has a Chance: Curly, Jack, and Bill (and Other Characters of the Hills, Brush, and Plains) (New York, 1994)

LIBRARY OF CONGRESS CATALOGING-IN-PUBLICATION DATA

Garry, Jim.
    Weapons of the Lewis and Clark expedition / by Jim Garry.
      p. cm.
    Includes bibliographical references and index.
    ISBN 978-0-87062-412-4 (hbk. : alk. paper)
    1. Lewis and Clark Expedition (1804–1806)—Equipment and supplies.
2. Firearms—West (U.S.)—History—19th century. 3. Weapons—West
(U.S.)—History—19th century. I. Title.
    F592.7.G37 2012
    917.804'2—dc23

2012003087

Contents

Illustrations

Preface

During the past twenty-five or thirty years, research on the Lewis and Clark expedition has spread from a cottage industry to a much more extensive field of work. Not surprisingly, all this research has revealed much information not known to the writers of fifty years ago. Nevertheless, no thorough, systematic examination of the Corps of Discovery's arsenal has been attempted for some time. Now, two hundred-plus years after Lewis began gathering munitions for the expedition, it seems a good time to reconsider the nature and significance of these important tools.

This book looks, piece by piece, at how the expedition was armed, how the military nature of the expedition affected the use of weapons, and how the weapons were cared for. It also offers a bit about the trade in guns among the tribes encountered. Each chapter looks at one of the major weapon types carried by the expedition. Some of the chapters are short because through time we have been left with little information about the weapon. Lost records are generally not the cause—rather it is because there were never any records to lose. Sometimes a tool was so commonplace that it needed no description. For instance, if we were making a comparable expedition today, how many of us would take the time to describe how we were taking notes, other than perhaps mentioning the use of a laptop computer? Anyone reading our accounts ten years from now would know exactly what was meant. In two hundred years the laptop computer may well seem as crude as the ink Lewis and Clark had to make as they "proceeded on." This lack of description of the obvious and commonplace is one of the great problems in historical research. And it is compounded by the fact that many records have not survived the years. Most of the records of the Harper's Ferry Arsenal were burned intentionally during the Civil War. Other records, in various archives, have been misplaced through the years. While lost records do surface on occasion, all researchers have a story comparable to William Stafford's poem, "An Argument Against the Empirical Method," which reads, in its entirety, "Some haystacks don't even have any needle."[1]

Other chapters present plentiful data, both from the journals and from previous research into particular types of weapons. Unanswered questions in these chapters are generally the result of the lack of records. There are two chapters in particular, one on Lewis's air gun and one on the short rifles, that have resulted in more spilled ink than the combined blood spilled by the expedition's weapons. About the short rifles, it can be said with a high degree of certainty that no one can say with any degree of certainty what they were. And there is more than a little dispute still going on about Lewis's air gun. More power to the arguers. They keep research alive and well.

Given the general lack of understanding about early nineteenth century firearms, I have included an appendix with a short history of their evolution and how the expedition's flintlocks worked. If you have extensive knowledge about firearms of the period, feel free to skip that section. If you aren't sure which end points down range, you might want to read that appendix first.

---

[1]William Stafford, "An Argument Against the Empirical Method," from *An Argument Against the Empirical Method*, 186.

Acknowledgments

A book of this type cannot be created without help. There are a number of people without whose assistance I could never have finished the research or the manuscript. Frances Clymer, Nathan Bender, Mary Robinson, Kurt Graham, and all the staff at the Buffalo Bill Historical Center's McCracken Research Library helped me through about 90 percent of the research. George Chalou, Brenda Kepley, Cynthia Fox, David Wallace, and a number of other staff members helped me to finish the rest of the research at the National Archives. Warren Newman and David Kennedy at the Buffalo Bill Historical Center's Cody Firearms Museum also offered assistance and consultation. Herman Viola, O. H. McKagan, Robert Pickering, Grace Mary Oates, and Sandy Nykerk read all or parts of the manuscript and offered valuable commentary. Sean Campbell at the Buffalo Bill Historical Center was most helpful in locating and accessing photographs, and Michael Carrick was indispensable, both in supplying photographs and especially in providing consultations about the weapons, the short rifles in particular.

To all of these people, and others who offered assistance, I offer a heartfelt thank-you.

Introduction

Thomas Jefferson, one of the Enlightenment's last gifts to the world, was a man of great vision and a dreamer of grand dreams. His magnificent home, Monticello, sat on the crest of the Appalachians, with civilization in the valley to his east and the frontier beginning in the valley to his west. His vision reached far to the east, where he drank in the learning of the great minds of Western civilization, and far to the west, where he saw in the distance, both in time and space, an enlightened, civilized country stretching all the way to the Pacific. Jefferson hungered for knowledge—a hunger some have likened to an infection—as only a man of the Enlightenment could. His desired to know that western land as it was, a realm of as yet unknown wild flora and fauna and, as he conceived it, unknown wild nations. Jefferson had dreamed of exploring the West most of his life, and during the last quarter of the eighteenth century, had actually hatched several schemes to do so. Once he was president, he began seriously to plan expeditions to survey the West. One such expedition should, he felt, follow the Missouri River to its westernmost headwaters, cross the Continental Divide, and then descend the Columbia River to the Pacific.

As well as being a great dreamer, Jefferson was a great talker. There is a tale, likely apocryphal, that John Kennedy, hosting a dinner for Nobel laureates at the White House, referred to the dinner conversation as the finest and most intellectual held there since Jefferson had dined alone. But Jefferson seems seldom to have dined alone while he was president. As a truly great talker, he equally loved to listen to good talkers: to discuss, to prompt, and to be prompted; to share in great conversation. We can only imagine how many dinner conversations at the White House touched on western exploration. It is known that his secretary, Meriwether Lewis, generally dined with him. Reading Lewis's letters and journals, one can see that he shared Jefferson's passion to explore the West. Indeed, it is possible that Lewis received his initial infection from the president. By 1803, Jefferson had decided that the western survey of the Missouri and the Columbia should be undertaken by his secretary, whose former job as an army payroll officer had taken him from one frontier fort to another. As a result, Lewis was a skilled wilderness traveler, for at the end of the eighteenth century the paths between the widely scattered posts were often not much more than game trails. He was also, for the time and place, well educated (though largely self-taught) and seems to have been a born researcher.

By the time Lewis left Washington in the early spring of 1803, the expedition was well planned. Jefferson and Lewis both knew that this trip, of long duration and into largely unknown country, would have to both feed itself off the land and be prepared to defend itself, so munitions of the first order were a top priority. It is not surprising that Lewis's first stop was at the brand-new federal arsenal at Harper's Ferry, Virginia.

In order to "provide for the common defense," every country must be able to arm itself, and avoid reliance on a foreign power (who may one day be an enemy) for the material of defense. Hence, every country not wishing to be in thrall to another must be able to manufacture its own arms and materials of war. The United States began to develop arsenals for the manufacture, repair, and storage of weapons during the Revolution. Because of the difficulty of transportation and security concerns, the arsenals were small and scattered throughout the states. Following the Revolution, when there was no longer a hostile army within its borders, the young country saw many advantages to centralizing the manufacture of weapons. The first large production arsenal was funded by Congress in 1794 and built at Springfield, Massachusetts, the following year.

In 1798 a second arsenal was built at Harper's Ferry, Virginia. Harper's Ferry was picked for three reasons. First, the young country needed more production facilities. Second, two separate facilities seemed safer from natural disaster and possible invasion than did a single expanded arsenal at Springfield. Third, for political reasons the facility needed to be in the South. Harper's Ferry met all necessary criteria. The river provided power equal to that available at Springfield, and it was far enough inland to be safe from coastal raids. And it was in the South.[1]

Carrying a letter of introduction from Secretary of War Henry Dearborn instructing the arsenal to provide all possible help, Lewis stayed long enough to make sure that the arsenal could supply him with knives, tomahawks, pipe tomahawks, and fifteen rifles and their accouterments, as well as that the collapsible iron-framed boat he had designed could be built to his specifications.

Once he was satisfied that Joseph Perkin, the arsenal superintendent, had all tasks well in hand, Lewis left for Philadelphia, where he appears to have been a whirlwind of activity. He divided his time between study and shopping. The leading lights of the young nation's intellectual community tutored Lewis in the skills he needed for the expedition. Andrew Ellicott and Robert Patterson coached him in math and the instruments needed to navigate and to fix latitudes and longitudes for the maps to be produced. Benjamin Rush both coached him on medicine and helped him put together his medical kit. Jefferson had already taught him much geology and anthropology, and had given him a lengthy questionnaire, prepared by Jefferson and such men as Rush, to help Lewis with ethnographic studies of the cultures he was going to meet. Lewis, already a first-rate

---

[1]By 1803 the arsenals other than these two were being converted to storage and repair facilities. During the Civil War, Harper's Ferry could not be protected from Confederate troops, so to prevent it falling into enemy hands, the Union Army burned the arsenal, with all its records.

botanist with a good knowledge of medicinal plants, received training in the new Linnaean method of cataloguing plants and animals to further his already considerable skills as a naturalist.

Lewis's shopping forays were designed to outfit an expedition of fifteen men for two years. He procured clothing, tents, packs, storage containers, cooking and dining utensils, powder and lead, trade goods and gifts for the tribes they would meet, study, and interact with—everything necessary for two years with little or no chance of resupply, once they left St. Louis.

From Philadelphia to Pittsburgh, always urged on by letters from Jefferson, Lewis worried his way through the summer. While his keelboat was being built on the Ohio River near Pittsburgh, Lewis returned to Harper's Ferry to test-fire the rifles and to pick up the equipment and supplies Joseph Perkin had prepared for him. Finally, with the level of the Ohio dropping as the summer wore on, Lewis loaded his weapons and supplies and shoved his keelboat into the current of the first of the major rivers he would run.

The keelboat itself may well have been Lewis's design. It certainly bore little resemblance to most of the keelboats seen on the waters of the West. The more or less standard design of such a boat was double-prowed, with steering sweep in the rear and anchor and tow-rope post in the bow. The cabin, if present, tended to be at midship. If the boat was outfitted with a mast, it might well rise from the cabin's roof. Lewis's boat, however, looked more like a Spanish river galley, with its cabin in the stern and its mast standing clear at midship. Different as it was from the standard, it was well designed and well built. Even in the low, late-summer waters of the Ohio it sustained no real damage from the many rocks it encountered. The fact that it often ran aground and had, on occasions, to dragged through riffles by oxen after having its load lightened by unloading says more about the condition of the Ohio in the days before dams than about the boat, which drew only two and a half feet of water.[2]

[2]Thomas Rodney, *A Journey through the West.*

The boat's deck was lined with storage lockers that were hinged so they could be tipped up to form breastworks if the vessel needed to be defended. The cabin was both sleeping and work space for the expedition's two officers, while an awning could protect the men from rainy nights. There was a galley for cooking and a square-rigged sail to take advantage of favorable winds. The boat was set up to allow a tow cable to be attached, the most effective means of moving it against the current of the Missouri. In effect, the keelboat was designed to be home and fort, as well as traveling warehouse to carry all the expedition's gear, supplies, and trade goods. Its aspect as a fort was reinforced when, while wintering near St. Louis, the captains added a cannon and two blunderbusses to its armaments.

Sometime between leaving Pittsburgh in the summer of 1803 and leaving St. Louis in the spring of 1804, the expedition changed its character if not its purpose. Though there is no surviving description of how and when the vision shifted, Lewis and his co-commander, William Clark, realized that they needed more men if they were going to do all that was asked of them. It seems likely that Jefferson's and Lewis's plan was originally influenced by two things. First, they were informed by the writings of Canadian explorers such as David Thompson and Alexander MacKenzie.[3] These two had traveled extensively in western Canada, and their treks included river trips to the Arctic and Pacific Oceans with small groups of men. They had been intent, not on diplomacy or scientific research, but on exploring new routes to the Pacific and, to a lesser extent, in making accurate maps. Second, Jefferson had dreamed of this expedition for so long that the idea of its needing to be small while passing through country to which the United States had no claim seems to have become fixed in his mind. Most of his

---

[3]David Thompson and Alexander McKenzie were exploring and mapping western Canada. Many writers, including Gary Moulton, suggest that McKenzie's *Voyages from Montreal through the Continent of North America to Frozen and Pacific Oceans* (London, 1801) was a push to Jefferson to try again for the expedition he had been dreaming of and planning for a quarter century. He had also been exposed to Thompson's maps.

conversations with Lewis had taken place prior to the Louisiana Purchase. They had probably envisioned the trip as a fast survey through territory claimed by European powers. But any serious diplomatic issues evaporated when Jefferson concluded the Louisiana Purchase, which included the entire Missouri River basin. Until the expedition crossed the Continental Divide, it would be in American territory. Even in the Columbia River drainage the United States had a claim. The Columbia River was named for the *Columbia Rediva,* a United States flagged vessel and the first ship to cross the dangerous bar at the Columbia's mouth and sail up the river. That Spain disagreed with this assessment and sent troops to try to stop the American expedition is a matter for a different discussion.

What is important for this study is that during the winter of 1803–1804, when Lewis and Clark organized and prepared their men for the expedition at Camp Dubois, the captains realized that to do all that was proposed would require a far larger expedition than originally planned.[4] Their contacts in St. Louis with traders and men knowledgeable of the Missouri tribes also suggested that a larger party would be safer on its way up the river. Between the spring of 1803, when Lewis left Washington, D.C., and the spring of 1804, when the Corps of Discovery headed west from St. Louis, the expedition tripled in size from its planned fifteen men. The two captains had to acquire more supplies and two additional boats, pirogues that required crews of six and seven. Acquiring the additional boats and learning more about the nature of the Missouri River led Lewis and Clark to hire at least a dozen *engagés,* professional boatmen who knew both the handling of boats and the character of the lower Missouri. They were hired to make the trip as far as the Mandan metropolitan area and were then to return to St. Louis with the keelboat in

---

[4]William Clark had given up his commission and was recommissioned for the expedition. However, his commission was as a lieutenant, not at his former rank of captain. Lewis was intent on having Clark as co-leader, not as his subordinate. Clark agreed with that plan, so the two men simply referred to Clark as "Captain," and the men apparently never knew otherwise.

1805. These extra men needed additional arms and ammunition. That Lewis and Clark acquired more ammunition while at Camp Dubois, but apparently made no effort to acquire additional rifles, suggests that many of the men recruited brought muskets or rifles with them. Probably acting on the advice of men familiar with trade on the Missouri, the captains did acquire a cannon and two blunderbusses with which to arm the keelboat, and later the pirogues and canoes. Some ammunition came from the same frontier forts that supplied at least seventeen of the men; some was apparently purchased in St. Louis.

The Corps of Discovery fired a salute with its swivel gun when it left Camp Dubois in the spring of 1804. It fired a salute with all guns when it returned to St. Louis in the fall of 1806. In between those two salutes, the Corps found daily uses for its guns.

The Corps ate off its rifles because, though the members of the expedition brought flour, corn, and other basics, and traded for Indian foods such as corn and camas, they were carnivores for the most part; they ate what they shot. When game was plentiful, as it was while the Corps crossed Montana during the summer of 1805, the party feasted. When the expedition's hunters shot nothing, as was often the case crossing the Bitterroots in the fall of 1805, the explorers began to count their tallow candles as part of their food stock. Assuming an average of two meals a day, we can estimate that the Corps ate 74,000 individual meals during the course of the expedition. As Lewis wrote,

> we eat an emensity of meat; it requires 4 deer, an Elk and a deer, or one buffaloe, to supply us plentifully 24 hours. meat now forms our food principally as we reserve our flour parched meal and corn as much as possible for the rocky mountains which we are shortly to enter, and where from the indian account game is not very abundant
>
> Lewis, July 12, 1805[5]

Consuming a buffalo a day seems like quite a lot to us. But for men struggling up the Missouri River in pirogues and dugout canoes, it was not. Voyageurs, the expert Canadian boatmen

---

[5]Moulton, *Journals of the Lewis & Clark Expedition*, 4:379.

working for the Hudson Bay and the Northwest companies during the period, served under contracts that often specified how much meat was to be provided. It was generally nine or ten pounds of meat per man per day. Considering that during the second summer in the West the Corps of Discovery was comprised of thirty-one men, a nursing mother, and a dog that weighed as much as some of the men, it does not seem unreasonable to imagine the group eating three to four hundred pounds of meat in a day, about as much as a cow buffalo would provide.

The captains placed great store in their "modern firearms," but many of the animals they encountered in the West were larger and tougher than the ones they knew in the East. For instance, the Corps discovered that there was a major difference between the black bears around which the men had grown up and the grizzlies they encountered in the West. To put it another way, their faith in their "modern firearms" was severely shaken by their encounters with grizzly bears:

In the evening the men in two of the rear canoes discovered a large brown bear lying in the open grounds about 300 paces from the river, and six of them went out to attack him, all good hunters; they took the advantage of a small eminence which concealed them and got within 40 paces of him unperceived, two of them reserved their fires as had been previously conscerted, the four others fired nearly at the same time and put each his bullet through him, two of the balls passed through the bulk of both lobes of his lungs, in an instant this monster ran at them with open mouth, the two who had reserved their fires discharged their pieces at him as he came towards them, boath of them struck him, one only slightly and the other fortunately broke his shoulder, this however retarded his motion for a moment only, the men unable to reload their guns took to flight, the bear pursued and had very nearly overtaken them before they reached the river; two of the party betook themselves to a canoe and the others seperated concealed themselves among the willows, reloaded their pieces, each discharged his piece at him as they had an opportunity they struck him several times again but the guns served only to direct the bear to them, in this manner he pursued two of them seperately so close that they were obliged to throw aside their guns and pouches and throw themselves into the river altho' the bank was nearly twenty feet perpendicular; so enraged was this anamal that he plunged into the river only a few feet behind the second man he had compelled take refuge in the water, when one of those who still remained on shore shot him through the head and finally killed him; they then took him on shore and butchered him when they found eight balls had passed through him in different directions.

Lewis, May 14, 1805[6]

As a former hunting guide, I feel compelled to comment on this story. It is the nature of hunters to feel confident of their aim. It is the nature of young men to be hesitant to admit failure. And it is important to remember that adrenaline strongly affects perception during an event and memory afterward. Of the first four shots fired at the resting bear, we may assume that at least one of the shots hit, as the bear was unlikely to get as upset as it did from the noise. Of the second two shots, the broken shoulder seems likely, as the writing suggests the bear went down momentarily. How the other hunter would know his shot only slightly injured the bear is impossible to understand. Assuming that the two who reached the canoe were unlikely to have a clear shot once the action moved above the cut bank, there were four men remaining in hiding in the willows, shooting as the opportunity presented itself. If we allow one shot each and then one last one for the head shot, that makes a minimum of eleven shots. While butchering the bear they found eight wounds. That means three misses. More importantly, there is no way of knowing whether any of the first volleys hit the lungs as suggested. But the story does hint at matters of interest to us.

"Forty paces," depending on Lewis's definition, is something between thirty-five and ninety yards. The upper half of those distances is pushing the range of accuracy for the Model 1795 muskets carried by the soldiers reassigned to the Corps and pushing the range for power both for the muskets and some of the small-caliber Pennsylvania rifles carried by the "nine young men from Kentucky." The only weapons available that were

---

[6]Ibid., 4:151.

possibly deadly for a grizzly at that range would have been the expedition's short rifles. Since none of the journals say anything about who was carrying what weapon at that encounter, it is impossible today to know what weapons were used. But it is worth thinking about the weapons involved in each of these hunting incidents when reading the journals.

Not only were bears an important food source but even more so a source of oil and fat. The bear in the above incident yielded "several gallons of oil." Old-timers I have worked with in the mountains relate that once you have used bear grease, lard and even butter pale in comparison. So, in spite of learning a healthy respect for the grizzlies, the Corps continued to hunt them at every opportunity. Only when a lone individual bumped into a bear did diplomacy take precedence over firearms, and as Lewis realized while standing thigh deep in the Missouri with only his espontoon for defense, the velvet glove of diplomacy works best when covering a steel fist. That understanding was even clearer when applied to the people the Corps met.

Diplomacy was one of the expedition's primary purposes. Lewis and Clark were to alert the tribes they met to the fact that the United States now owned Louisiana. The new nation was not only the new political power along the river, but was determined to become the dominant trading power. Putting oneself forward as the new "owner" of the lands the tribes had occupied for generations stretching back through the mists of time required a fine touch of diplomacy. The captains certainly saw to the fact that the velvet glove did not hide the steel fist, the military nature of the expedition. Every tribe the Corps met, even those who had not seen white people before, had seen firearms. Guns were one of the most sought after trade items in the West.

There were times, even during a trip devoted to science and diplomacy, when the diplomatic glove had to be removed. When the expedition met the Teton Sioux, the glove came off. Certainly the fact that both sides had learned all they knew of the other through contact with each other's enemies affected this

first meeting. Obviously, the Tetons were reluctant to give up
their position controlling the flow of trade up and down the
Missouri. Aside from losing the profitable middleman position
in the river trade, what the Americans were proposing meant the
arming of the Teton's up-river enemies. So it is not surprising
that diplomatic meetings between the Corps of Discovery and
the Tetons went badly.

The first and most serious confrontation, on September 25,
1804, involved the leaders of a large group of the Tetons testing
the Corps. They attempted to stop Clark and a boatload of men
from shoving off from the bank of the Missouri by seizing the
pirogue's cable as one of the chiefs laid hold of Clark. Within
moments the Teton received a determined answer. Clark had
drawn his sword, his men had prepared for a fight, and the
men on the other pirogue and the keelboat had stood to with
personal weapons and the swivel gun and blunderbusses, loaded
and aimed. The confrontation ended without violence, and the
expedition moved on up the river. It seems that the Corps of
Discovery's large number of weapons and the men's obvious
willingness to use them may well have been what prevented a
fight that afternoon.

There are elements of the Corps of Discovery's planning that
are amazing. For instance, how could two such imaginative individuals as Thomas Jefferson and Meriwether Lewis, consulting
the best minds in the United States, have neglected to include
an artist in the Corps's roster? Future expeditions proved that
there were plenty of talented artists capable of making such a
trip. But they did think of practical matters. Lewis brought
extra gun locks and other spare parts, as well as a blacksmith
shop. Besides all the tools a blacksmith would need, the Corps
carried a forge along as far as the mouth of the Marias River in
Montana so that the equipment could be repaired and rebuilt.
But tools alone would not answer the Corps's needs. Broken
firearms might have served as a bluff against Indians, but they
would not have fed the expedition. Both Lewis and Clark wrote

separately that had it not been for the spare parts, and the talents of John Shields, they would have been in dire straits, with few if any working guns. Shields was one of the "nine young men from Kentucky," recruited off the frontier specifically for their wilderness skills. The captains had indeed recruited a wizard to accompany them to the Pacific and back.

Lewis took along an air rifle with which to impress Indians they were visiting. The magic of the air gun was that it worked without expensive gunpowder. All the tribes the Corps of Discovery encountered had been exposed to guns and the trade in guns. The expedition journals all refer to Indian guns. But none of them, in their writing at least, draws the obvious conclusion that North America was tied together with trade networks, as intricate as a spider's web, enabling the dispersion of goods and knowledge across the Far West as rapidly as it spread through Europe's "civilized" countries.

The purpose of the expedition was to carry the flag west, to explore and map the main river of the new Louisiana Purchase, to see if there was a practical route up the Missouri and down the Columbia to the Pacific, to strengthen the United States claim to the Columbia basin, to make scientific observations and to collect specimens of new species, and to contact the tribes both for science and diplomacy. The expedition's weapons were no more than tools. But they were the tools without which none of the other tools could have been used. They are the tools that fed and protected the men for twenty-nine months, from the time they left Camp Dubois with a cannon salute until they announced their return to St. Louis with a volley.

CHAPTER I

Model 1795 Musket

It was a beautiful, sunny afternoon along the Missouri River in the late summer of 1804. Whites and Indians were meeting to talk and to trade—not an unusual sight along the river. But at this meeting, talk was the more important of the two. Meriwether Lewis, William Clark, and the Corps of Discovery were representatives of the latest white government to claim the river and all the lands it drained. They were there to explain that claim and the new trade relations that would go with the new rule. The white men had announced their arrival with the big gun mounted on their keelboat, and the tribe now gathered on the bluffs above the river. Drawn up on the bank were the keelboat and two accompanying pirogues, the three vessels appearing to hold several tons of goods. About thirty men moved around the vessels, preparing to camp and, any river tribe would assume, to trade. The men were all armed, rifles and muskets either carried or near to hand.

More impressive to the tribe were the men on the bluff in front of them. One of the leaders, in splendid uniform and accompanied by his interpreter, stood with the tribal leaders. On the open ground in front of them the other leader, also in gold-braided uniform, drilled a group of uniformed men armed with polished muskets and gleaming bayonets. These white men obviously represented a major power. Never before had the tribe seen a military parade, or a group so well armed and trained to fight as a unit. The Corps was larger than the groups of white traders the tribes were used to seeing on the river, and the number of guns the group had demonstrated its power. The large cargo held the promise of future trade, and the parading of uniformed troops made an impressive show. The tribes waited, curious to hear the words that followed the show—a show that would be repeated with each large group of Indians the Corps encountered that summer.

The expedition's journalists refer only to parading the troops for the Indians. There is no explanation of how the parades were conducted. One can speculate from another reference. Lewis and Clark and the men who came from regular army units learned parading or drill from the same book, Baron von Steuben's *Regulations for the Order and Discipline of the Troops of the United States.*[1] Von Steuben used the word "parade" in two senses. First he called what would usually be referred to today as a parade ground a "parade," a term he also used to describe what the *Oxford English Dictionary* refers to as "an assembling or mustering of troops for inspection or display; esp. a muster of troops that takes place regularly at set hours, or at extraordinary times to hear orders read, as a preparation for a march, or any other special purpose." Lewis and Clark apparently used "parade" to mean the same thing as "drill" meant to von Steuben. To march and countermarch fifteen to twenty men, all armed with bayoneted muskets, perhaps even ending the drill with a volley from the muskets. This would certainly have been impressive, especially to people who had never seen such a display.

At least seventeen of the men of the Corps of Discovery were transfers from other army units. There is some evidence that a party of transfers dispatched to join Lewis along the Ohio was sent without weapons. They arrived after Lewis had already passed on his way downriver toward the Mississippi and thus

---

[1]Baron von Steuben, a Prussian, came to America to assist the rebels' cause during the Revolution. He became George Washington's inspector general, helped train Washington's army, and wrote, perhaps with the help of Jean-Baptiste Ternant, *Regulations for the Order and Discipline of the Troops of the United States.* Lewis and Clark had both used the book while on active duty before the expedition. The men who joined the Corps of Discovery from regular army units would also have been trained with this manual; an updated version was still the U.S. Army's drill manual in 1803.

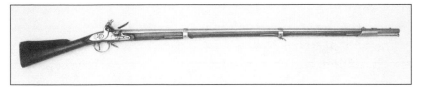

MODEL 1795 SPRINGFIELD MUSKET

This was the standard U.S. Army musket of the late eighteenth and early nineteenth centuries. Its inspiration was the 1760s patterns of muskets produced by France's Charleville Royal Manufactory, familiar to the Americans from during the Revolutionary War. *Courtesy Buffalo Bill Historical Center, Cody, Wyoming, U.S.A.; Gift of Olin Corporation, Winchester Arms Collection, 1988.8.1603.*

failed to become part of the expedition.[2] Upon reaching Camp Dubois, Lewis and Clark were in an area where the unit commanders were not only known to them but were, for the most part at least, their friends. On the whole, these captains sent good men to the Corps and sent them with all their gear.

These men would have been armed not with rifles but with muskets. Before discussing the muskets, something should be explained. The United States Army musket at the beginning of the nineteenth century was one that went into production at the Springfield Arsenal in 1795, and while today these muskets are referred to as Model 1795 muskets, they were not designated thus by the army but by gun collectors during the twentieth century. If you are interested in title designations, I would refer you to such writers as Norman Flayderman,[3] whose expertise includes collecting and the designations that go with collecting. But the name is in common usage, so, with apologies to purists, let us proceed.

The late eighteenth century's equivalents of today's M-16 and AK-47 were England's Land Pattern muskets (the famous Brown

---

[2]Jackson, *Letters of the Lewis & Clark Expedition*, items 28:37 and 98:144.
[3]Flayderman, *Flayderman's Guide to Antique American Firearms*, 536–38.

Bess) and France's Charleville Royal Manufactory's models. During the American Revolution, it was easier for the new army of the United States to acquire Charleville weapons, and after the Revolution the army still favored muskets of the Charleville pattern. In 1795 the Springfield Arsenal began making muskets on either the Charleville 1763 or 1768 pattern, depending on which of the various authorities one believes (which of course is the reason for the designation later applied to the weapon by collectors). The arsenal at Harper's Ferry also began to produce Model 1795 muskets, but not until 1801. The U.S. versions of the Charleville types were patterned after the French model, but changes and improvements were constantly being made. There was no required standardization between Springfield and Harper's Ferry, so each made improvements independently.

All the various models of the Model 1795 were roughly five feet long and could mount a triangular bayonet of about fifteen inches. The barrels were smooth bored, around forty-five inches long, with a bore of .69 caliber.[4] Gunpowder of the period was not clean burning. So much powder residue collected inside the barrel during a battle that by its later stages it was impossible to force a .69 caliber ball into the barrel. The result was that the Model 1795 had to fire a ball of only .63 caliber, the caliber of standard-issue ammunition and bullet molds. Since armies distributed musket balls and powder in paper cartridges, soldiers used the paper as wadding to attempt to size the ball, using all, part, or none of the paper as wadding, depending on how many rounds had been fired—a method that did not work all that well. The ball tended to ricochet down the barrel, and its direction of flight was determined by the vector of its last contact with the bore. This inherent inaccuracy was so acknowledged and accepted that the Model 1795, like most muskets of the period, did not even have a rear sight, and the front sight was obscured by the bayonet. Why would the army of America, a country

---

[4]Caliber is a decimal measurement in inches; i.e., .69 caliber is .69 inches.

that prided itself on its riflemen, arm its soldiers with muskets? Because then, as now, volume of fire more than accuracy of fire was how an army dominated a battlefield.

In European-style battles of the period, accuracy was less important than the volume of lead. These battles were fought at relatively close range, with gunpowder that produced dense clouds of smoke that obscured the enemy. Well-trained troops could fire about four rounds from muskets in the same amount of time it took a riflemen to fire one. Four volleys fired at massed troops obscured by smoke was likely to be more effective than the second volley of riflemen blinded on a smoke-filled battlefield.

During the Revolution, the ranger companies of George Washington's army were equipped with rifles. Since those ranger companies had performed well, and since the new country was well supplied with riflemen trained from early childhood, the army decided to make use of that pool of riflemen. The new U.S. Army was reorganized into the Legion of the United States in 1792. Each sub-legion included a battalion of four rifle companies of eighty-two men each. But in 1796 there was a further reorganization, and the rifle companies were dropped. During the period from the end of the Revolution until the opening of the Springfield Arsenal in 1795, the army was supplied with arms purchased from Europe and with arms made, under government contract, by American gunsmiths. Most of the European and contract weapons were shelved at the army's storage arsenals or recycled to militia units as the production of the two U.S. manufacturing arsenals filled the army's needs. All evidence points to the fact that by 1803 regular army troops were not equipped with rifles but with Model 1795 muskets made at either Springfield or Harper's Ferry.

Of the approximately seventeen men who came to the Corps of Discovery from other army units, five were artillerymen from Capt. Amos Stoddard's company; eleven were infantrymen from the three infantry companies commanded by the Bissell brothers and John Campbell; and one (John Potts) came from Capt. Robert

Purdy's company. Another five men (Frazer and MacNeal—who are referred to at least once each in the journals as being armed with muskets—and Goodrich, Reed, and Werner) may or may not have been in the service when they joined the Corps. Lewis's and Clark's journals both refer to some men possessing muskets and bayonets. This reinforces the idea that the men transferred to the Corps brought their muskets and equipment with them.

The officers published their "Detachment Order" on April 1, 1804, naming twenty-seven noncommissioned officers and men as part of the "Perminent Detachment" that would accompany them to the Pacific and back. This would indicate that over the course of the year since Lewis had left Washington, the size of the party had doubled from his original intention. Hence we may assume the roughly fifteen sets of arms and gear Lewis had obtained before his departure were already on a ration list, as the "Detachment Order" states that four other men "are to be treated in all respects as those men who form the Permonant detachment, except with regard to the advance of Pay, and the distribution of Arms and Accoutrements intended for the expedition."[5] The Corps needed every issue musket and private rifle available to supplement the fifteen rifles Lewis brought from Harper's Ferry.

The party's journalists were woefully inadequate at recording specifics about their firearms. Lewis and Clark often distinguished smooth-bore from rifled weapons by using the terms "musket" and "rifle." But they were as apt to use the nonspecific term "gun." Clark, for instance, on May 10, 1804, writes that he "order every man to have 100 Balls for ther Rifles & 2 lb. Of Buck Shot for those with mussquets."[6] Issuing buckshot would seem to indicate that, at least at the beginning of the expedition, the muskets were seen as defensive weapons not to be used for hunting. Later that would change. The Corps had ball ammunition for the muskets as well, since on August 25, 1805, Lewis commented in his journal, "This morning while passing through the Shoshone

---

[5]Moulton, *Journals of the Lewis & Clark Expedition*, 2:187–88.
[6]Ibid., 2:213.

cove Frazier fired his musket at some ducks in a little pond at the distance of about 60 yards from me; the ball rebounded from the water and passed within a few feet of me."[7] The fall before, on October 4, 1804, Clark referred to a group of Indians who, trying to get the party's attention and urge them to land, took the measure of skipping a musket ball in front of the boats as well as yelling to the men. As Clark noted in his journal, "we were obliged to Drop down 3 miles to get the Chanel Suft. Deep to pass up, Several Indians on the Shore viewing of us Called us to land   one of them gave 3 yels & Sciped [skipped] a ball before us, we payed no attention to him, proceeded on."[8] Proceeding on showed admirable restraint, since this occurred in the realm of the Teton Sioux just a week after two confrontations that almost led to war between the tribe and the Corps.

The Model 1795s came closest to real combat during those two confrontations with the Tetons on September 25 and 28, 1804. The Corps had arrived in the Teton country anticipating trouble. Based on reports they had received in the St. Louis area and from tribes lower down the Missouri, the Tetons were expected to be belligerent. So it was not surprising that on September 24, having already had some trouble with them over the Corps's horses and expecting a formal meeting with them the next day, Lewis wrote, "we prepared Some Clothes and a fiew meadels for the Chiefs of the Teton's hand [band] of Seaux which we expect to See to day at the next river . . . prepared all things for action in Case of necessity."[9]

On September 25, everyone in the Corps was locked and loaded, the Model 1795s most probably loaded with buckshot, the best load for defense and close combat. Clark's account indicates that all hands were ready for action.

> Envited those Cheifs on board to Show them our boat and Such Curi-
> ossities as was Strange to them, we gave them 1/4 a glass of whiskey

---

[7]Ibid., 5:168.
[8]Ibid., 3:142.
[9]Ibid., 3:107.

which they appeared to be verry fond of, Sucked the bottle after it was out & Soon began to be troublesom, one the 2d Cheif assumeing Drunkness, as a Cloake for his rascally intentions   I went with those Cheifs [NB: in one of the Perogues with 5 men 3 & 2 Ints.][10] (which left the boat with great reluctiance) to Shore with a view of reconseleing those men to us, as Soon as I landed the Perogue three of their young men Seased the Cable of the Perogue [NB: in which we had presents &c.], the Cheifs Soldr. [NB: each Chief has a Soldier] Huged the mast, and the 2d Chief was verry insolent both in words & justures [NB: pretended drunkenness & staggered up against us] declareing I Should not go on, Stateing he had not recved presents Suffient from us, his justures were of Such a personal nature I felt my Self Compeled to Draw my Sword, [NB: and made a Signal to the boat to perpar for action] at this motion Capt. Lewis ordered all under arms in the boat, those with me also Showed a Disposition to Defend themselves and me, the grand Chief then took hold of the roop & ordered the young warrers away, I felt my Self warm & Spoke in verry positive terms

Most of the warriers appeared to have ther Bows Strung and took out their arrows from ther quves. as I [NB: being surrounded] was not permited [NB: by them] to return, I Sent all the men except 2 Inpt. [interpreters] to the boat, the perogu Soon returned with about 12 of our detumined men ready for any event   this movement <in the 1s instance after Landing Pointed their arrows blank &c. which> caused a no: of the Indians to withdraw at a distance, [NB: leaving their chiefs soldiers alone with me] Their treatment to me was verry rough & I think justified roughness on my part, they all left my Perogue and Councild. with themselves   the result I could not lern and nearly all went off   after remaining in this Situation Some time I offered my hand to the 1 & 2 Chief who refused to recve it. I turned off & went with my men on board the perogue, I had not progd. more the 10 paces before the 1st Chief 3rd & 2 Brave men waded in after me. I took them in & went on board <prd on 1 me &>

we proceeded on about 1 mile & anchored out off a willow Island placed a guard on Shore to protect the Cooks & a guard in the boat, fastened the Perogues to the boat, I call this Island bad humered Island as we were in a bad humer.

Clark, September 25, 1804[11]

---

[10]The comments designated [NB:] are, to quote Gary Moulton, "Nicholas Biddle's emendations or interlineations." *Journals of the Lewis & Clark Expedition,* 3:113.

[11]Ibid., 3:113–14.

In his first set of notes, Clark actually stated his men's "Disposition to Defend themselves and me" in more direct words. He wrote, "the few men that was with me haveing previously taken up their guns with a full determination to defend me if possible."[12] Further on in the passage, when Clark refers to the twelve men returning to shore prepared for action, it is easy to imagine a dozen soldiers carrying buckshot-loaded muskets with fixed bayonets. A dozen men with bayoneted muskets, backed up by more than thirty with rifles, muskets, two blunderbusses, and the swivel gun would have certainly been a warlike enough aspect to assure the Tetons that even if they won the fight their losses would have been unacceptable (since every warrior lost to the Tetons meant that there was a family without a hunter, a serious condition for a family dependent on the buffalo for food, shelter, clothing, trade, and more).

Three days later, in an incident that does not seem to have impressed either Lewis or Clark but that made Joseph Whitehouse think they were about to be in a war, Lewis trained the swivel gun on a group of Tetons holding the keelboat's cable and told the men to prepared to fire on the group.

> we draged the river in hopes to find our anker but it was in vain.   about 9 oClock we went to Set off   Some of the chiefs was then on board and concluded to go a little ways with us.   when we were about to Shove off a nomber of warries on Shore caught hold of our cable and another whiped of[f] the children   the women went off also   only about 60 warries on the edge of the bank and we just under the bank. Some of them had fire arms and the rest had Good bows and arrows ready for war. the consequences had like to have been bad as Capt. Lewis was near cutting the cable with his Sword and giving orders for the party to fire on them. then the chiefs went out and Spoke to them.   they Said if we would Give them a carrit of tobacco they would loose the rope.   we gave them tobacco.   the chief after Some hesitation loosed the rope himself. we then Set of[f] under a fine breese of wind.
>
> *Whitehouse, September 28, 1804*[13]

---

[12]Ibid., 3:112.
[13]Ibid., 11:89–90.

Whitehouse's concern rose from the spectacle of some sixty warriors armed with firearms and strung bows on a bank above the boat. Lewis and Clark may have read the mood of the Tetons differently than Whitehouse and not considered it worth mentioning in their journals, but both incidents could easily have gotten out of hand and turned into combat.

While the Corps clearly favored rifles for hunting, they equally recognized the value of muskets both for use and for trade. Having working firearms was critical to the expedition's very survival. Without guns they could not defend themselves against either hostile natives or grizzly bears and, more important, they could not feed themselves. But safety included insurance. The keelboat had returned to St. Louis from the Mandan villages in the spring of 1805. At the Great Falls of the Missouri the Corps had to cache their pirogues, which were too big to portage around the falls and to navigate the upper river. Some supplies, including arms and ammunition, were cached there and a short distance downstream, at the mouth of the Marias, so that, if things went desperately wrong farther along, the retreating men could resupply at those points. As Lewis noted:

> in order to guard against accedents we thout it well to conceal some ammunicion here and accordingly buryed a tin cannester of 4 lbs of powder and an adequate quantity of lead near our tent; a cannester of 6 lbs. lead and an ax in a thicket up the S. Fork three hundred yards distant from the point.   we concluded that we still could spare more ammunition for this deposit   Capt. Clark was therefore to make a further deposit in the morning, in addition to one Keg of 20 lbs. and an adequate proportion of lead which had been laid by to be buryed in the large Cash.   we now scelected the articles to be deposited in this cash which consisted of 2 best falling axes, one auger, a set of plains, some files, blacksmiths bellowses and hammers Stake tongs &c.   1 Keg of flour, 2 Kegs of parched meal, 2 Kegs of Pork, 1 Keg of salt, some chissels, a cooper's Howel, some tin cups, 2 Musqets, 3 brown bear skins, beaver skins, horns of the bighorned anamal, a part of the men's robes, clothing and all their superfluous baggage of every discription, and beaver traps.
>
> *Lewis, June 10, 1805*[14]

---

[14]Ibid., 4:275.

Another cache held the blunderbusses and more ammunition. Still another held the swivel gun. Aside from having more stores than they could carry in the canoes they had built during the winter to take the place of the keelboat on the upper Missouri and above, the makeup of the caches points out the value placed on rifles versus muskets. The truth was that the captains felt they could do without muskets more easily than rifles.

In spite of the decision to cache weapons, the expedition (in what some would call characteristically American fashion) seems never to have felt that it had enough guns. The Corps actually traded for a musket on April 20, 1806, and Lewis acquired one during the fight with the Blackfeet on July 27, 1806. They, of course, traded off muskets, too, including the one for which Lewis had traded. Once they had left the Missouri tributaries, horses became critical to the success of the enterprise—and horses were not cheap. Aside from normal trade goods, guns, powder, and lead were needed to acquire horses: the twenty-nine they got from the Shoshones and the Salish on their way west and that many more from various tribes on their way back. When the Corps had to trade guns to acquire needed horses or guiding services, the captains preferred to trade pistols and muskets, and even Lewis's personal shotgun, rather than rifles. On one occasion, Clark swapped his personal rifle, apparently temporarily, to one of his men so that he could trade that man's musket for the last horse needed to cross the Bitterroots.

As already mentioned, the Corps had numerous encounters with grizzly bears. Unfortunately, none of the journalists recorded what weapons were involved in any of the shooting incidents, so one can never know the exact reasons why some grizzly bears died quickly while others chased men considerable distances after being shot numerous times "in the vitals." But educated guesses are possible. For instance, how effective was the Model 1795 against what Lewis called the "variegated" bear? The Model 1795 fired a ball weighing slightly less than an ounce. A ball that big lost power quickly once it left the barrel. At twenty or thirty yards, it was devastating. At one hundred yards it had lost enough power to enrage rather than seriously injure a grizzly, even if the shooter hit the precise target, not a guaranteed outcome with a musket. There is no evidence in the journals of anyone figuring out which guns were good at what range when hunting the big bears. Instead, the Corps determined how many men should be involved in a fight with a grizzly or, as they often called them, a "white" bear.

> we saw also many tracks of the white bear of enormous size, along the river shore and about the carcases of the Buffaloe, on which I presume they feed.   we have not as yet seen one of these anamals, tho' their tracks are so abundant and recent.   the men as well as ourselves are anxious to meet with some of these bear.
>
> *Lewis, April 13, 1805*[15]

Their first meetings did nothing to change that attitude.

> it is a much more furious and formidable anamal, and will frequently pursue the hunter when wounded. it is asstonishing to see the wounds they will bear before they can be put to death. the Indians may well fear this anamal equiped as they generally are with their bows and arrows or indifferent fuzees, but in the hands of skillfull riflemen they are by no means as formidable or dangerous as they have been represented.
>
> *Lewis, April 29, 1805*[16]

That attitude changed for some members of the Corps over the next few days. Only a week later Lewis wrote,

> I find that the curiossity of our party is pretty well satisfyed with rispect to this anamal, the formidable appearance of the male bear killed on the 5th added to the difficulty with which they die when even shot through the vital parts, has staggered the resolution [of] several of them, others however seem keen for action with the bear; I expect these gentlemen will give us some amusement shotly as they soon begin now to coppulate.
>
> *Lewis, May 6, 1805*[17]

By June 2, Lewis's own judgment had changed. After several men had shot a grizzly, "Drewyer finally killed it by a shot in the

[15]Ibid., 4:31.
[16]Ibid., 4:84–85.
[17]Ibid., 4:118.

head; the [NB: only] shot indeed that will conquer the farocity of these tremendious anamals."[18] And ten days later, on June 12, Lewis finished this first analysis of the grizzly: "here we met with two large bear, and killed them boath at the first fire, a circumstance which I beleive has never happened with the party in killing the brown bear before."[19]

One of the rules of hunting dangerous game, such as the grizzly, is that one should try to break bone. That means either a front leg or the back to "anchor" the hard-to-kill animal and to keep it from getting at the hunter. At close range, the Model 1795 with its large ball would have been a fine weapon for that, the large ball giving it enough force (foot pounds of energy) to give it good stopping power. However, given the inaccuracy of the musket at longer ranges and the fact that its ball's energy dropped off so quickly, it could not be thought of as a good weapon for bears.

The one time there is a record of a musket being used in a confrontation with a grizzly, the musket was not fired. On July 15, 1806, Lewis and his part of the then split expedition were at the Great Falls of the Missouri. Lewis wrote, "Dispatched McNeal early this morning to the lower part of portage in order to learn whether the Cash and white perogue remained untouched or in what state they were." Lewis thought no more of MacNeal that day; his mind was occupied with fear for George Drouillard, who was off looking for lost, possibly stolen, horses in prime grizzly bear habitat. As Lewis wrote, "I had already settled it in my mind that a whitebear had killed him and should have set out tomorrow in surch of him, and if I could not find him to continue my rout to Maria's river. I knew that if he met with a bear in the plains even he would attack him. and that if any accedent should happen to seperate him from his horse in that situation the chances in favour of his being killed would be as 9 to 10."[20] Drouillard returned safely but without the seven missing

---

[18]Ibid., 4:242.
[19]Ibid., 4:280.
[20]Ibid., 8:109.

horses. Lewis wrote nothing about the lost horses. The Corps was not dependent on those horses, but Lewis did depend on Drouillard. While Lewis was ready to start his Marias exploration, he waited, since

> McNeal road one of the horses which I intend to take and has not yet returned.   a little before dark McNeal returned with his musquet broken off at the breech, and informed me that on his arrival at willow run [NB?: on the portage] he had approached a white bear within ten feet without discover him the bear being in the thick brush, the horse took the allarm and turning short threw him immediately under the bear; this animal raised himself on his hinder feet for battle, and gave him time to recover from his fall which he did in an instant and with his clubbed musquet he struck the bear over the head and cut him with the guard of the gun and broke off the breech, the bear stunned with the stroke fell to the ground and began to scratch his head with his feet; this gave McNeal time to climb a willow tree which was near at hand and thus fortunately made his escape.   the bear waited at the foot of the tree untill late in the evening before he left him, when McNeal ventured down and caught his horse which had by this time strayed off to the distance of 2 ms. and returned to camp.
>
> *Lewis, July 15, 1806*[21]

Adrenalin is an amazing drug. To hit a grizzly hard enough to put it down, even temporarily, is a remarkable feat. Hitting the bear gave McNeal the time to climb and the impetus to do so. Had he shot it at that range, he probably would not have killed it instantly and might have made the mistake of waiting to see the shot's effect before starting to climb. In that scenario he probably would not have climbed high enough to escape even a severely wounded and very enraged bear. Though he rendered his musket into scrap iron and kindling wood, he saved his life. And in a few days he was able to replace the musket with one of the two muskets recovered from one of the downstream caches.

The word "musket" is used fewer than fifty times in the journals, and some of these are references to Indian weapons. It is important to remember that the Corps of Discovery was a military unit. To the officers and many of the men the musket was

---

[21]Ibid., 8:110.

a standard and acceptable weapon. The muskets were so much a part of the men's world that they used musket balls as a unit of measure. Men referred to hailstones the size of musket balls and to edible roots that size. While its accuracy as a hunting weapon was well below the rifle's, the men would have been accustomed to the weapon and to have internalized its limitations as well as its strengths to the point of having thought it a very good modern firearm that they were happy to have with them. This attitude is no different from that of the hundreds of today's hunters who hunt deer and black bear with shotguns, smooth bored like the Model 1795 musket. It only means knowing the limits of the weapon and the hunter. Probably the limited number of references to muskets merely indicates their ubiquity. Most likely muskets were taken so much for granted that the journalists felt little need to mention them, just as a journalist today would hardly mention each time he used his pocket knife.

CHAPTER 2

Swivel Gun and Blunderbusses

It was spring of 1804 along the confluence of the three great rivers of our young country's West. Meriwether Lewis had come down the Ohio, the westward flowing of the three, the summer and fall before. He and William Clark had established their winter quarters on the east bank of the Mississippi, both to keep their men away from the temptations of St. Louis and because, technically, St. Louis was still a French city when they arrived in the area. Those who have not spent time in the area think of the nineteenth-century Mississippi Valley in terms of Mark Twain. But Lewis and Clark were there two generations before the birth of Huckleberry Finn. Twain described what Huck and Jim saw as they drifted down the Mississippi—big woods along a big river with occasional towns, villages, and plantations dotting the banks. At the beginning of the century, when Lewis and Clark wintered there, there were very few settlements. Other than a few larger settlements, like St. Louis, civilization still amounted to small islands scattered through the wilderness, mainly along the streams. If the Corps of Discovery's winter camp is thought of as one of those islands, it must be remembered as no more permanent than a sand bar in the Mississippi.

On a rainy day in mid-May 1804, the Corps of Discovery bade farewell to Camp Dubois at the mouth of the Wood River, where they had come together as a unit. The keelboat and the two accompanying pirogues, carrying over forty men, headed across the Mississippi and up the Missouri on their way to the Pacific. The men saluted their departure by firing their small cannon.

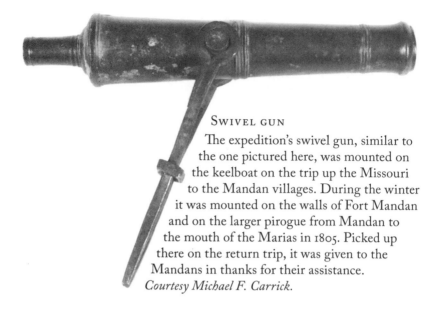

SWIVEL GUN
The expedition's swivel gun, similar to
the one pictured here, was mounted on
the keelboat on the trip up the Missouri
to the Mandan villages. During the winter
it was mounted on the walls of Fort Mandan
and on the larger pirogue from Mandan to
the mouth of the Marias in 1805. Picked up
there on the return trip, it was given to the
Mandans in thanks for their assistance.
Courtesy Michael F. Carrick.

There is no evidence that any representatives of the many tribes
they would meet, or of any of the tribes west of the Mississippi,
heard the cannon. But it announced the arrival of a new culture
that would sweep like a flood behind these explorers.

There is no surviving evidence that Lewis acquired any firearms other than the short rifles he picked up at Harper's Ferry
and the pistols he bought in Philadelphia. There is also no evidence that, before leaving the East, he anticipated any particular trouble with the tribes he expected to meet. In St. Louis,
though he would have heard stories from the traders dealing
with the tribes along the Missouri River of trouble with the
Teton Sioux, who occupied a trade bottleneck beyond which
travel by the traders was difficult at best. The Corps would hear
similar tales about the Blackfeet during the next winter at Fort
Mandan. The Tetons wanted to maintain their position as the
prime trading middlemen between St. Louis traders and the
upriver tribes. That meant that white traders going up the river

had to be prepared to trade only with the Tetons, pay them a tariff to pass through their lands, or make such a show of force that the Tetons would not try to stop them.

Lewis and Clark, intent on establishing the authority of the new controlling white power of the Louisiana country, were probably not anxious to pay a tariff, thus recognizing the dominance of the Tetons over the United States. They certainly were not going to negotiate with the Tetons for all the merchandise that they had purchased as trade goods. That meant that they had to rely on diplomacy, and the captains seem to have understood that diplomacy works best when backed up with force. Lewis and Clark, between the summer of 1803 and the spring of 1804, had doubled the size of their permanent party and tripled the size of the group for the first year. They had worked with the officers they knew along the frontier to get good men transferred to the Corps of Discovery and to make sure that the men brought their weapons and equipment with them. They had talked to men such as René Auguste and Jean Pierre Chouteau, who were experts in the upriver trade. If they were going to bring off a show of force to make their diplomacy more effective, not only more guns but bigger guns were called for. There are enough records of small cannons and blunderbusses along the frontier and the Missouri during the early nineteenth century to suggest that Lewis and Clark would have had no trouble acquiring them in the St. Louis area. The journals don't mention where the expedition acquired the heavier weapons, but they do reveal that the Corps left Camp Dubois with two blunderbusses and a small cannon mounted on the keelboat.

The cannon they had was not what leaps to most people's minds when they hear the term.

What Lewis and Clark had acquired was a salute or swivel gun. In his 1816 *Military Dictionary*, Charles James describes the swivel as "a small piece of ordnance which turns on a pivot or swivel."[1] Though this description is hardly helpful, Harold

[1] Quoted in Peterson, *Encyclopedia of Firearms*, 314.

Peterson explains that while any firearm mounted on a pivot qualifies technically, "In the usual context it refers to a small cannon, the trunnions of which are permanently mounted in an iron yoke. The trunnions are free to move in the yoke so the gun may be elevated or depressed in aiming. The lower part of the yoke is termed the pivot, and this fits into a hole bored in a timber."[2] In the case of a keelboat, the hole would usually be bored in either the stern or bow post. From the various journal accounts, it is known that the Corps mounted its swivel on the bow of the keelboat.

The first mention of the swivel is in Joseph Whitehouse's journal on May 14, 1804: "We fired our Swivel on the bow hoisted Sail and Set out in high Spirits for the western Expedition."[3] William Clark's January 21, 1804, sketch of the keelboat, detailed enough to show the anchor, does not show the swivel mounted. Clark did write a letter in April of 1804 stating that additional arms had been mounted on the keelboat.[4] These two references may be seen to suggest that the idea of adding more and heavier armament was made as more information about the Missouri River tribes, the Teton Sioux in particular, became available. There are enough references to swivel guns in the literature of the fur trade to indicate that such weapons were obtainable in the St. Louis area.

The journals do not describe the weapon in any detail, but all swivel guns had certain things in common. They were small, muzzle-loading cannons, two and half to three feet long. Some had a handle a foot or so long extending from the back to aid in aiming, others had a simple ball-shaped handle on the back similar to those on larger cannons of the period. Swivels were smooth bored and loaded like a musket. They were fired by lighting powder that had been poured into the touch hole, a small hole bored in through the top of the barrel into the back of the gun's bore. The device used to ignite the powder in the touch hole was a

---

[2]Ibid., 314, 315.
[3]Moulton, *Journals of the Lewis and Clark Expedition*, 11:1.
[4]Jackson, *Letters of the Lewis and Clark Expedition*, item 112:175–76.

slow match, a smoldering fuse that carried a glowing ember at its end. That glowing end was touched to the powder to fire the gun.

It was the mounting of these small cannons, too large to be hand held when fired, that gave them the name "swivel." A swivel had a pair of studs, forged as part of the barrel, on either side at the balance point. These studs fit into a Y-shaped yoke with holes to accommodate the studs at the top of each of the upper arms. The lower arm of the Y was a long, round rod. The rod was designed to be inserted into a hole bored for it in a solid, heavy base, such as the bow post of the keelboat or a heavy post in a fort wall. This arrangement allowed the swivel to be tilted within the forks of the yoke and then panned by twisting the rod of the yoke's lower arm within the hole in the mounting post.

What is known about the expedition's swivel is that the weapon was almost certainly a one-pounder (bored to accept a one-pound lead ball, roughly 1⅔ inches in diameter). This can be determined from John Ordway's journal. He recorded in the journal that during the confrontation with the Teton Sioux, on September 25, 1804, the swivel was loaded with sixteen musket balls. The Model 1795 musket's bore was .69 caliber, or 14 gauge.[5] But the Model 1795 used .63 caliber balls, or 18 gauge, so sixteen balls is slightly less than a pound.

Three days later, during a somewhat less spectacular confrontation (three Teton warriors were holding the anchor cable, attempting to prevent the keelboat's departure until they received more tobacco), Clark wrote, "I threw a Carot of Tobacco to is Chief Spoke So as to touch his pride   took the port fire from the gunner   the Chief gives the Tobaco to his Soldiers & he jurked the rope from them and handed it to the bows man."[6] "Port fire" is another name for the slow match used to fire the swivel. Clark was either making sure the gunner did not fire

---

[5]Gauge, according to Peterson's *Encyclopedia of Firearms*, is the measurement used today for shotguns, while caliber is used for rifles. Gauge measures gun bore diameter by the number of lead balls of that size it would take to weigh one pound. For example, the 14 gauge mentioned here means that fourteen .69 caliber balls would weigh one pound.

[6]Moulton, *Journals of the Lewis and Clark Expedition*, 3:124.

without sufficient cause or he wanted the chief to know how close they were to shooting. If Clark was calling the Tetons' bluff, the swivel was a bigger hole card than his sword would have been.

The swivel was not fired on either of those occasions. But it is easy to believe that the swivel and two blunderbusses, all three of which would have appeared to have huge bores, helped the expedition's persuasiveness. Those were the only times the swivel was loaded in anger. The rest of the time it found service as a salute cannon. There are seventeen clear references to its being fired, every time to salute a village, to celebrate such holidays as Christmas, New Year's Day, or the Fourth of July. For example, Clark wrote on July 4, 1804, that the men, "ussered in the day by a discharge of one <discharge> shot from our Bow piece."[7] On Christmas Day of 1804, Clark wrote that he was "awakened before Day by a discharge of 3 platoons [meaning volleys] from the Party and the french, the men merrily Disposed, I give them all a little Taffia and permitted 3 Cannon fired, at raising Our flag, Some men went out to hunt & the Others to Danceing and Continued untill 9 oClock P,M, when the frolick ended &c."[8] The three cannon he refers to are likely the swivel and the two blunderbusses.

Both the swivel and the two blunderbusses were cached at Great Falls. According to the journals, "the Swivel we hid under the rocks in a clift near the river a little abov our lower camp."[9] There were two reasons for leaving the swivel gun. The first was that, as with the blunderbusses, the captains felt they were past the danger zone. The only tribes from which they feared possible armed confrontations were the Tetons and the Blackfeet. They were well past all the Sioux tribes and thought that, past Great Falls, they were past the Blackfeet territory. The second reason was a bit more prosaic. The Corps no longer had a vessel large enough to accommodate the swivel. The red pirogue, the only vessel that had come up the river past Fort Mandan that was large

---

[7]Ibid., 2:347.
[8]Ibid., 3:261.
[9]Ibid., 4:334.

enough to mount the swivel, was being cached. Firing it from the white pirogue or any of the canoes would have at least cracked, if not ripped out, the bow or stern where it was mounted, capsized the boat, and likely caused serious injury to anyone behind it.

When the expedition returned to the caches at Great Falls, they found the red pirogue to be in a state of decay. The swivel gun was thus useless, which made it an ideal gift. Lewis and Clark had intended to reward the Mandans for their help and friendship by giving them all their horses when they returned from the Pacific. Lewis abandoned his horses near the mouth of the Marias; they could make better time on the river. He feared his group that had explored the Marias was being pursued by the Blackfeet after his fight with a party of them. Clark, who had most of the horses during his trip down the Yellowstone, lost about half of them, probably to the Crows, while his men were building canoes to finish their exploration of the Yellowstone. Clark assigned three men to take the remaining horses overland and to meet the rest of the Corps at the Mandan villages. Their first night out, the Crows took the rest of the horses. Sergeant Pryor and his men had to walk back to the river, build bull boats (willow frames covered with buffalo hides) and follow Clark down the river. So when the Corps returned to the Mandan settlements without the horses, Lewis and Clark decided to give them the swivel gun instead.

> as our Swivel Could no longer be Serveceable to us as it could not be fireed on board the largest Perogue, we Concluded to make a present of it to the Great Chief of the Menetaras (the One Eye) with a view to ingratiate him more Strongly in our favour . . . I then a good deel of Ceremony made a preasent of the Swivel to the *One Eye* Chief and told him when he fired this gun to remember the words of his great father which we had given him.   this gun had announced the words of his great father to all the nations which we had Seen &c. &c.   after the council was over the gun was fired & delivered, the Chief appeared to be much pleased and conveyed it immediately to his village &c.
>
> *Clark, August 16, 1806*[10]

---

[10]Ibid., 8:303–304.

Clark exaggerated when he told One Eye that the gun had "announced the words . . . to all the nations," since it had been cached before the Corps met the Shoshones, the first tribe they met past the Mandans.

Ironically, and doubtless unintentionally, the gift of the cannon strengthened trade ties between the Mandans and St. Louis. The swivel gun was a gift of great prestige. One reason for that was that it was an expensive item to use, taking as it did a half pound of powder to fire one pound of lead. The swivel gun given to the Mandans was a one-pounder that required eight ounces of powder for each shot—enough to fire sixteen rounds from a Model 1795 musket. To be able to fire a salute from something like the swivel gun when others came to trade indicated that the owner was wealthy and powerful. One Eye would have rightly felt that the cannon was an important and useful gift.

Lewis and Clark gave up the swivel before meeting the Tetons on their return trip, which could have left them vulnerable in case of a confrontation. But the Corps was a hardier and a smarter group than they had been two years earlier, and had the advantage of being headed downstream. There was no diplomatic reason to stop and visit the Tetons, so the expedition did the sensible thing. They covered many miles every day, trying to pass through the Tetons' country as quickly as possible. The strategy worked. The only contacts the Corps had with the Tetons were some verbal exchanges as they passed. So the swivel gun passed from the history of the Corps of Discovery into the history of the Mandans, living up to only one of its names, "salute gun."

While the swivel gun was the expedition's artillery, the Corps also carried shoulder-fired heavy weapons. Probably at about the same time they acquired the swivel gun, Lewis and Clark acquired two blunderbusses. Since most people today have had no contact with blunderbusses outside cartoons, it might be well to start with a definition. The blunderbuss is "a short firearm with an expanding bore, usually flaring out in a bell at the muzzle. The name is believed to be a corruption of the German *Dunder*

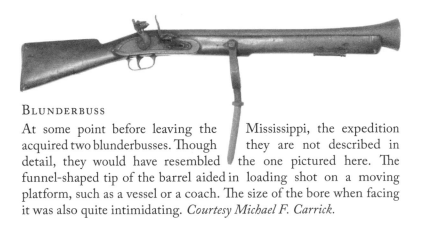

BLUNDERBUSS

At some point before leaving the Mississippi, the expedition acquired two blunderbusses. Though they are not described in detail, they would have resembled the one pictured here. The funnel-shaped tip of the barrel aided in loading shot on a moving platform, such as a vessel or a coach. The size of the bore when facing it was also quite intimidating. *Courtesy Michael F. Carrick.*

(thunder) and *Buchse* (gun)."[11] The weapon, intended to fire shot rather than a single ball, was developed in Europe, probably in the early to middle seventeenth century. The blunderbuss's wide, flared muzzle is often thought to help scatter the shot, but in fact it does not, though this assumption reigned through most of the period of the weapon's use. The real and practical reason for the belled muzzle was that it facilitated loading. The weapon was designed for use on a rolling ship's deck or rocking coach: it is obviously easier to pour powder and shot into a three-inch funnel than into a barrel two-thirds of an inch across. It is also quite likely that looking down the throat of a gun with an apparent two- to four-inch bore is more intimidating than one with a half-inch bore.

Blunderbusses came in a variety of sizes, from those easily held and fired, similar to today's sawed-off shotguns, to those that were too big to be fired without a swivel to hold them. These larger ones were designed to be mounted on vessels or fort walls. Many of the smaller types, designed for coaches, ships, and home defense, still had a swivel attached to them so they could be mounted in the manner of the larger ones, or dismounted and

---

[11]Peterson, *Encyclopedia of Firearms*, 57, 58.

fired from the shoulder. The larger ones, according to Harold Peterson's *Encyclopedia of Firearms*, could hold up to 20 buckshot pushed by 120 grains of powder, and even a smaller one would have a bore as large as or larger than a Model 1795 musket and was capable of firing a dozen or more buckshot pellets at a time.[12] On a river trip such as the Corps of Discovery's, even small blunderbusses would have been considered particularly efficient defensive weapons.

The expedition's journalists left no detailed descriptions of the blunderbusses, but there are bits and pieces of information that hint at what the blunderbusses were. The earliest reference I have found to them is in an April 1804 letter from Clark to Lewis: "If 2 muskets were hung on Swivels in the Stern [of the keelboat] it would be well."[13] Since in America at the time the words "blunderbuss," "carbine," and "musketoon" were often used interchangeably, and since Clark's spelling was eccentric at best, it is certainly reasonable to assume that "musket" was his best attempt. The next month, when the Corps was a week into the trip from Camp Dubois, Patrick Gass seemingly referred to the blunderbusses and swivel gun when he wrote that they fired a three-gun salute in response to the town of St. Charles giving them three cheers as they departed. Gass actually uses the word "guns," while Joseph Whitehouse, on the same day, refers to firing the swivel as a salute. Most likely, the other two guns would have been the blunderbusses.

The journals also tell us of the uses to which the blunderbusses were put: to fire salutes and to frighten the Tetons during the 1804 confrontation. They were cached below Great Falls on the outward journey, and one was stepped on and broken by a buffalo. That incident, on the night of May 28 and 29, 1805, created a great deal of excitement and havoc in the camp. A bull buffalo swimming across the river arrived at their camp to find his way blocked by the white pirogue. He climbed over the pirogue

---

[12]Ibid., 57, 58.
[13]Jackson, *Letters of the Lewis and Clark Expedition*, item 112:175, 176.

and ran through the camp. Several men narrowly avoided being stepped on; the rifle of York, Clark's slave, and a blunderbuss were damaged. From this report we know that at least one of the blunderbusses was swivel mounted. The buffalo, according to Lewis's journal, "had also broken the spindle, pivit, and shattered the stock of one of the bluntderbushes on board."[14] Of course, John Shields was able, as always, to repair the damage. Clark does not say if the blunderbuss was mounted on the pirogue or lying on the deck or shore.

According to the journals, the red pirogue could mount the swivel gun, and either of the pirogues and probably the canoes could mount the blunderbusses. Clark wrote of mounting weapons on the keelboat when he discussed adding them to the arsenal. All of the journalists referred to the two blunderbusses as though they were the same, and the buffalo incident indicates that at least one of them had a swivel. If one had a swivel and the other did not, logic suggests that at least one of the journalists would have drawn the distinction.

During the winter at Fort Mandan, the swivel gun and both blunderbusses were used on several occasions to fire salutes. Given the military thought at the time, especially since Clark was an artillery officer and there were five artillerymen in the Corps, it seems likely that the fort walls were designed to accommodate the swivel gun and the blunderbusses, probably in more than one location each. The swivel for a blunderbuss would have been roughly the same as that of the swivel gun, save that rather than studs forged onto the barrel to connect the weapon to the yoke, there would have been a pin that ran through the gun's forearm. A metal yoke, a Y-shaped piece like the swivel gun's, was attached to the blunderbuss with its pin. The walls at Fort Mandan were made of pickets, and it would have been logical to drill several holes to accommodate the swivel and blunderbusses. Dowels could have been used to seal these holes against snow and ice when the guns were not mounted.

---

[14]Moulton, *Journals of the Lewis and Clark Expedition*, 4:215.

By the time the Corps headed into the upper Missouri, above the Great Falls, it had cached its heavy weapons, the swivel and both blunderbusses. Apparently the Corps had changed not only its makeup since it left St. Louis, but its view of the West as well. Lewis and Clark seem to have felt that they were leaving the land of the Blackfeet as they passed Great Falls and that there was no group beyond them that constituted a trade bottleneck. Sans such a tribe, there was little likelihood that they would run into anyone who would contest their passage. They expected to be welcomed from that point onward. There were times on the rest of the trip when the men "stood to" and were prepared to fight, but these were times when they feared petty theft, or perhaps grand larceny, not a war.

The Corps retrieved its heavy weapons on its way back. Given the fact that Lewis had just had his fight with the Blackfeet, I suspect they were loaded as soon as they were deemed clean. The blunderbusses made it all the way back to St. Louis. The last clear reference to them was when the Corps approached St. Charles, a short distance above the mouth of the Missouri. The expedition saw the people of the town on Sunday promenade.

> at 4PM we arived in Sight of St. Charles, the party rejoiced at the Sight of this hospital village plyed thear ores with great dexterity and we Soon arived opposit the Town, this day being Sunday we observed a number of Gentlemen and ladies walking on the bank, we Saluted the Village by three rounds from our blunderbuts and the Small arms of the party, and landed near the lower part of the town.
>
> *Clark, September 21, 1806*[15]

There was a last salute as the Corps arrived at St. Louis on September 23, 1806, when, according to Clark's journal, "we Suffered the party to fire off their pieces as a Salute to the Town."[16] This would have certainly included the blunderbusses if they had been reloaded after the salute at St. Charles. There was a practical reason for this as well as the expression of joy by young

---

[15]Ibid., 8:369.
[16]Ibid., 8:370.

warriors returning home. Firing off their weapons was an easy way to make them safe in town, where they were not likely to be needed. Firing a flintlock is much easier than pulling the ball with a screw.

The limited evidence suggests that the two blunderbusses were sold along with other gear as surplus goods at the end of the trip, to help defray costs of the expedition.[17] This was, after all, an army expedition, and the costs had to be reported to Congress. The expedition had cost more than had been anticipated. Even if someone had recognized the gear's historical significance, it would have been outweighed by the need to balance the books if at all possible. In reality, there is no evidence that anyone thought the means of the expedition was as important as the resulting notes, maps, and collected artifacts. As a result, the blunderbusses, along with many other pieces of equipment we would like to know more about today, vanished into the vastness of history and probably the West. The only people who wanted such pieces were probably planning a trip up the Missouri themselves. The fact that Lewis and Clark were able to purchase blunderbusses before the trip, and easily sell them after, suggests that the weapons were in demand among those interested in the Missouri River trade.

---

[17]Jackson, *Letters of the Lewis and Clark Expedition*, item 277:424.

HARPER'S FERRY MODEL 1803 RIFLE

The Model 1803 was the U.S. Army's first short rifle. One theory holds that the Harper's Ferry Arsenal produced a prototype of this rifle for Lewis to take on the expedition. *Courtesy Michael F. Carrick.*

CHAPTER 3

Short Rifles

Meriwether Lewis was secretary to the president of the United States when he was given command of the expedition up the Missouri River to the Continental Divide and on to the Pacific. Those ties to the president, coupled with the letter of instruction from the secretary of war to the superintendent, ensured that he received every assistance at the Harper's Ferry Arsenal. Aside from constructing the metal frame for a collapsible boat Lewis designed to use west of the Continental Divide and providing knives, tomahawks, and needed tools, the arsenal supplied Lewis with fifteen "short" rifles and their accouterments.[1]

From the end of the expedition until the last couple of decades of the twentieth century, everyone who studied the expedition accepted the conventional wisdom about what those short rifles were. Lewis was at Harper's Ferry in the spring and summer of 1803. The Harper's Ferry Arsenal made the Model 1803 Rifle, the U.S. Army's first short rifle. Although it seemed obvious that Lewis took fifteen of this newly designed rifle, research over the last fifteen years suggests that this was not the case. The Model 1803 rifle is named for the year it was designed. A proof model of the Model 1803 was sent to the secretary of war for approval in late November or early December of that year, and production of the rifles did not start until the second quarter of the 1804 fiscal year.[2] By then Lewis and Clark had been encamped at

---

[1] Jackson, *Letters of the Lewis and Clark Expedition*, item 54:75.
[2] The Harper's Ferry Arsenal's fiscal year ran October 1 to September 30, according to Brown, *Guns of Harper's Ferry*, 44.

Camp Dubois on the east side of the Mississippi River for many weeks. In the summer of 1803, when Lewis departed Harper's Ferry with his rifles, the proof model of the Model 1803 was still several months away from being completed. To understand what Lewis may have obtained from Harper's Ferry, it is important to understand the history of American military rifles.

At the beginning of the nineteenth century, the debate about whether the military should arm its troops with muskets or rifles dated back over a century and a half, to the creation of the first rifles. The argument was over whether accuracy or rate of fire was more important. A rifle is more accurate, but to achieve that accuracy a rifle of the flintlock period required a ball that was very close to the same size as the bore. The ball was placed in a lubricated patch and forced down the barrel. "Forced" is not an exaggeration, and it was the patch's lubrication that helped make forcing the ball down the barrel possible. A musket was smooth bored and fired a ball several thousandths of an inch smaller in diameter than the bore. For that reason, loading a musket was faster, allowing the firing of up to four rounds for each rifle shot. Armies therefore preferred muskets. But what the musket offered in firing volume was lost in accuracy. The accepted military wisdom of the late eighteenth and early nineteenth centuries was that on a smoke-filled battlefield, where one could not see the enemy clearly, a higher volume of fire was more deadly. But Americans loved and cherished their rifles. At least on the frontier, the direction the new country faced philosophically, the rifle both fed and protected the citizens. During all our wars in the eighteenth century the rifle had been important to American history, and perhaps more important, it had become part of the country's mythology. As a result of the rifle's importance, the U.S. Army faced a dichotomy in military thinking, a dichotomy that was reflected in various reorganizations of the army during the decades following the Revolution.

After the Revolution there were no units in the regular army equipped with rifles. The army was reorganized in 1792 from four infantry regiments and one light dragoon squadron into the "Legion of the United States." There were a number of "sub-legions," each of which was to include a battalion of four eighty-two-man rifle companies. That created a supply problem. While the military had a number of armories for the storage and repair of weapons, the country's only arsenal designed for large-scale manufacture of weapons was at Springfield, Massachusetts. The Springfield Arsenal did not have the tools to build rifles at that time, and the army needed about two thousand—immediately.

Though large factories for manufacturing rifles would develop during the nineteenth century, in the eighteenth century gun making was a cottage industry, with a major center around York and Lancaster, Pennsylvania. The army contracted to have two thousand rifles made by Pennsylvania gunsmiths. These guns are generally designated by today's collectors and arms historians as the 1792 Contract Rifles. There are few if any known to exist today, and they are hard to identify, since they look like a typical Pennsylvania rifle of the period.[3] They were designed with a full-length stock, a 44½-inch barrel (changed to 42 inches before the contract expired) and bored at .42 caliber. The caliber was quickly changed to .48 or .50. The .02-inch difference may indicate a difference in measuring the bore in the lands (ridges) or grooves.[4]

A total of 1,476 of these rifles were delivered to the army before the next reorganization in 1796. In that reorganization the rifle

---

[3]The term "Pennsylvania rifle" comes from the center of the manufacturing area for the rifles. Southeastern Pennsylvania was where the design was perfected and where most of the gunsmiths working in the tradition at that time were trained. Most of them stayed in the area and helped create a school of design as well as an industry. During the period, virtually all nonmilitary weapons were produced by small firms or single gunsmiths, each producing only a few rifles each year. In other words, gun manufacturing was a cottage industry whose product changed over both time and distance. Pennsylvania was not the only region making guns during the period, and a knowledgeable person of the time could recognize both where a particular type of weapon was made and during which generation, if not which decade. Such rifles are also called "Kentucky rifles."

[4]Measurements can be made across the bore diameter and give two different calibers. The measurement across the lands, the bore's inner diameter or across the grooves, the spiral cuts for the rifling, gives slightly different calibers.

companies were dropped, and the army found itself with 1,476 rifles it did not need. So it stored them at its arsenals and armories. But in 1796 none were stored at Harper's Ferry, because in 1796 there was no arsenal at Harper's Ferry. Three years later, when Congress again authorized the formation of a rifle regiment, the arsenal at Harper's Ferry was only partially built. As it turned out, the rifle regiment never materialized, but the War Department did pursue the design and construction of a new rifle for the army.

During the last few years of the eighteenth century, the United States balanced on the brink of war with France, but there were two other foreign powers to worry about as well: Spain to the new country's south and west and England, seen as a fermenter of Indian troubles in the Northwest and occasional impressor of sailors at sea. The young country recognized the need for another arsenal to match the one at Springfield. For political and logistical reasons the new arsenal needed to be in the South, and for security reasons the new arsenal needed to be far enough inland to be immune from naval gunfire and amphibious attack. Harper's Ferry was such a site.

In 1798 Joseph Perkin was appointed superintendent, and construction of an arsenal began. Shops and housing were built first, and during the first two years, while the canal and water wheels to power the plant were being constructed, the new shops were used for reconditioning arms sent there from the arsenals at Shepardstown, Carlisle, Philadelphia, and New London. Records show that Perkin's people began fabricating weapons in 1800. Stuart Brown notes that, while rumors of a Model 1800 rifle have been around for some time, there is no evidence of such a rifle being built. Instead there appear to have been some Pennsylvania Rifles repaired with lock plates made at Harper's Ferry.[5] Merritt Smith is less sure. He claims that "A small quantity of full stocked rifles may have been made at Harper's Ferry on an experimental basis in 1800 & 1801."[6] There are no surviving rifles

---

[5]Brown, *Guns of Harper's Ferry*, 28, 29.
[6]Merritt Smith, *Harper's Ferry Armory and the New Technology*, 52–57.

or descriptions of any made at Harper's Ferry in 1800 or 1801, and the lists of Harper's Ferry manufactures that survive in the National Archives show no rifles made before 1804. Since the records published may be a bit vague, it is necessary to recognize a degree of uncertainty at the possibility of such arms existing. Beginning in 1804 the records become comparatively clear. The Harper's Ferry records that could answer all these questions were destroyed in 1861, when the Union Army burned the facility to prevent its falling into Confederate hands.

Brown points out that Henry Dearborn, secretary of war in 1803, wrote to Joseph Perkin in May that there was "a deficiency of rifles in the public arsenals," but also that the rifles on hand were not "as well calculated for actual service as could be wished." Dearborn also stated that it was "considered advisable to have a suitable number of judicially constructed rifles manufactured at the [Harper's Ferry] Armory" under Perkin's direction, and directed that the "necessary measures for commencing the manufacture" of the rifles be taken "as soon as may be after completing the muskets now in hand."[7] This was the War Department's pursuit of a new rifle for the army. And it was as radical a switch for the military as the one from the .30 caliber to the .223 caliber a century and a half later.

As regards design, the arms to which both the military and civilian riflemen had become accustomed were the American "long rifles," now generally referred to as "Kentucky rifles." However, as Donald Jackson noted in his *Letters of the Lewis and Clark Expedition with Related Documents, 1783–1845,* Dearborn had "such convincing proof of the advantage of short rifles . . . over the longs [commonly used] in actual service as to leave no doubt in [his] mind of preferring the short rifle, with larger calibers than the long ones," and of preferring "stiff steel ramrods instead of wooden ones. . . . The great facility which such rifles afford in charging in addition to their being less liable to become fouled by firing, gives a decided advantage to men of equal skill and

---

[7]Brown, *Guns of Harper's Ferry,* 29.

dexterity over those armed with the common long rifle."[8] There seem to have been two reasons that Dearborn favored shorter barrel length. First, since the patched ball for a rifle had to be strenuously forced down the length of the barrel, the longer the barrel, the more time it took to load. Second, since most of the fouling occurred in the last few inches of the barrel, the theory was that a shorter barrel produced less fouling.

Dearborn's letter was written four or five weeks after Lewis left Harper's Ferry for Philadelphia. Lewis returned the first week of July to pick up all the items prepared for him by the arsenal, and on July 7, Lewis test fired the rifles. In other words, Perkin had one month from the receipt of Dearborn's letter to work with whatever was on hand. And what work might they have done, based on Dearborn's letter and Lewis's discussions with Perkin? It must be considered that, as the president's secretary, Lewis may have been privy to discussions with Dearborn or his staff while the ideas expressed in the letter were forming.

The first possibility is that Harper's Ferry built the rifles for Lewis from scratch. While most records of the arsenal were destroyed during the Civil War, some documents, mainly ones sent to the War Department, have survived. The lists of arms manufactured at Harper's Ferry from 1798 to 1800 show no muskets or rifles. In 1801 the lists show 293 muskets and no rifles. The 1802 production was 1,472 muskets and no rifles. Again, the lists for 1803 show that 1,048 muskets were made, but no rifles. The same lists also show no pattern rifles were made that year, yet correspondence with Secretary of War Dearborn indicates that the pattern rifle for the Model 1803 was approved in December, remembering that the arsenal's fiscal year began on the first of October. Further, the arsenal didn't purchase the first 216 stock blanks from Abraham Sheppard, a contractor supplying wooden products to the arsenal, until the October–December quarter of fiscal year 1804, early enough to make the pattern rifle but too late to have made any for Lewis. On the other hand, destruction

---

[8]Jackson, *Letters of the Lewis and Clark Expedition*, item 54:75.

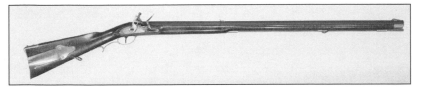

SHORTENED 1792 CONTRACT RIFLE

This replica of the model has been shortened and had the sling added in the manner suggested by one theory of what the Harper's Ferry Arsenal produced as a short rifle for the expedition. *Courtesy Michael F. Carrick.*

of the Harper's Ferry records during the Civil War leaves the possibility that some records are missing.

A second scenario is that the arsenal modified existing weapons. There were arms and military stores from several federal repositories that had been transferred to Harper's Ferry in 1800. These various shipments included some of the 1792 contract rifles. The journals suggest that the fifteen rifles Lewis obtained were of the same caliber. For instance, when Lewis was accidentally shot in August of 1806, the ball that injured him, while it pierced both of his upper thighs (buttocks), remained in his trousers. When he recovered it, he observed, "the ball had lodged in my breeches which I knew to be the ball of the short rifles such as he [Cruzatte] had."[9] The 1792 contract rifles were of the same size, probably .50 caliber.

What modifications would have been likely? Perhaps most critically was the replacement of the rifles' locks. In 1795 the government purchased 3,000 locks from John Ketland, an English manufacturer with offices in America. These were made to exact specifications that allowed interchangeability. Perkin's gunsmiths certainly had the ability to do any necessary modifications to fifteen rifles that would have allowed the use of these locks. This idea is reinforced by two facts, that Lewis took a

---

[9]Moulton, *Journals of the Lewis and Clark Expedition*, 8:154–56.

number of extra locks and that there were several journal references to John Shields replacing damaged locks.

Lewis notes that he received fifteen "gun slings" from the military stores at Harper's Ferry, the same number as the number of rifles prepared for him. Since the 1792 contract rifles were not designed for slings (nor was the Model 1803 or any of those left over from the Revolution), it suggests that the rifles were modified to accommodate them. Given the quality of the workmen at the arsenal, adding sling swivels to the rifles would have been no major task. Slings would have made the rifles much easier to carry. On April 12, 1806, the journals indicate that the captains had the men with short rifles take them along during a portage on the Columbia River when they feared theft of goods. If the rifles had not had slings, half of the available work force would have been working one handed, something unlikely to have been ordered when all hands were needed for the heavy work of ferrying supplies around rapids.

Then there is the big question: why Lewis and all the other journalists refer to them as "short rifles." The use of the word "short" is the reason that, for the better part of two centuries, people assumed that Lewis had obtained Model 1803 rifles—the United States Army's first designated short rifle. The Model 1803 had a thirty-three-inch barrel. Most Pennsylvania rifles of the period had barrels from forty-two to forty-eight inches. The 1792 contract rifles had barrels of either forty-two or forty-four and a half inches, depending on when in the contract period they were made. If there were no Model 1803 rifles that could have been made before Lewis left Harper's Ferry, then there are two possible explanations for the use of the descriptive "short."

The first is that all were 1792 contract rifles made late enough in the contract period to have forty-two-inch barrels and that length was enough shorter than the men's personal Pennsylvania rifles and the Model 1795 muskets' forty-four-inch barrels to merit the "short rifle" title. The second possibility is that Perkin shared Dearborn's thinking about shorter rifle barrels, or quickly saw the advantages when Dearborn wrote to him about it. Either way, this line of reasoning suggests that the gunsmiths at the arsenal cut down the barrels of the rifles they were modifying.

To be done properly, the barrels of any rifles had to be cut off at the breech. Joseph Perkin had brought fifteen skilled gunsmiths from the New London Arsenal, most of whom had apprenticed in the Pennsylvania Rifle gunsmithing tradition. Given the quality of such workmen, cutting down the barrels and stocks would not have been a significant problem. This is entirely possible, and perhaps the most likely answer to the short rifle question. One might even suggest that these were prototypes of the Model 1803 pattern rifle produced a few months later. Certainly, whatever modifications were made were satisfactory, since Lewis seemed well pleased when he test fired them on his return to Harper's Ferry to pick up the rifles and other supplies.

There have been additional suggestions about where Lewis might have acquired the short rifles. George Moller argues, "It is far more likely that the expedition left Pittsburgh with rifles that had been obtained from Schuylkill Arsenal along with the expedition's other equipment during the spring of 1803."[10] Schuylkill, a military arsenal at Philadelphia, was established as a storage and repair center, not a manufacturing arsenal such as Harper's Ferry or Springfield. While Lewis did obtain some equipment from Schuylkill, the evidence for his obtaining rifles there is missing and actually contradicts Lewis's letter to Thomas Jefferson, written in Lancaster, Pennsylvania on April 20, 1803: "My Rifles, Tomahawks & knives are preparing at Harper's Ferry, and are already in a state of forwardness that leaves me little doubt of their being in readiness in due time."[11]

Another suggestion that has been made is that Lewis managed to get rifles built to the needs of the expedition while he was in Philadelphia. Certainly there were plenty of excellent gunsmiths in that part of Pennsylvania, and certainly there are pieces of

[10]Moller, *American Military Shoulder Arms*, 2:337, 338.
[11]Jackson, *Letters of the Lewis and Clark Expedition*, item 28:40.

the expedition's records missing. But between the journals and letters referring to Harper's Ferry preparing the short rifle, and no mention being made of any dealings with gunsmiths in Pennsylvania, this seems most unlikely.

When dealing with an array of possibilities, it is wise to apply Occam's razor to cut through the confusion. William Occam, a fourteenth-century English scholastic philosopher, postulated that the simplest viable explanation is usually the proper one. This razor has been used by scientists for the last seven hundred years as a tool to help cut through complicated problems. The key to using the razor is to remember the all-important word: viable. Using this process, it seems that we must conclude that, unless missing records from Harper's Ferry or some other concrete evidence of a prototype Model 1803 surfaces, Lewis received some existing rifles, modified by the skilled craftsmen of Harper's Ferry.

Readers of Gary Moulton's excellent edition of *The Journals of the Lewis and Clark Expedition* should be aware that Moulton is not a weapons historian. He did rely on what for years were considered the standard reference volumes on Lewis and Clark weapons, Carl P. Russell's *Firearms, Traps, and Tools of the Mountain Men* and his *Guns of the Early Frontiers: A History of Firearms from Colonial Times through the Years of the Western Fur Trade*. These were written before the round of research begun by such scholars as Stuart Brown, Jr. So, when reading Moulton (and, if you are truly interested in the expedition, you must read Moulton), forget his references to the Model 1803 rifle. It is impossible, two hundred years after the fact, to know exactly what rifles Lewis obtained at Harper's Ferry. Unless . . .

. . . somewhere in the National Archives in Washington, D.C., there is a document that could answer this question. On February 12, 1808, Samuel Annin, the military storekeeper at the Harper's Ferry Arsenal, wrote to the War Department, "enclosing a return of Arms manufactured from commencement of the Establishment to 31 Dec, '07." Unfortunately, the microfilm on which this is recorded has the envelope containing the document and the cover letter quoted above, but not the document itself. After searching in vain through the various departments that might have been interested enough to have had the return moved to their files, I believe that there are only two possible explanations. Either the document is lost or it is misfiled. The stack of papers in which it resided was moved many times in the more than a century and a half between its original filing and its being microfilmed sometime in the mid-twentieth century. During at least one of those moves, someone dropped the stack. Pages were separated when the stack was reassembled, and the document began a slow drift through the currents of the archives. I have devoted all the time I plan to searching for that document. The next time you have a few days to spare while working at the National Archives, feel free to resume the search. It may or may not be of any help in answering the question of what rifles Perkin "prepared" for Meriwether Lewis.

Since the permanent party of the expedition numbered thirty, why did Lewis only requisition fifteen rifles? It has been suggested that there was not time to prepare—modify—more than that. When one looks at the total equipment list from Harper's Ferry and Philadelphia, it seems that Lewis was still thinking in terms that he and Jefferson had discussed—i.e., that a group of two officers and ten or twelve men would make the trip. It was during the trip down the Ohio and at Camp Dubois that he and Clark realized that the party would have to be at least twice that size. While Lewis and Clark seemed to have been able to have at least doubled their ammunition supply and acquire the swivel gun and blunderbusses while at Camp Dubois, there is no indication of their trying to acquire more rifles. Either there were none to be had at a price they could afford or they felt they had enough. Assuming that the nine young men from Kentucky, Lewis, Clark, York, Drouillard, and perhaps part of the engagés had personal rifles and that the men from the army's frontier companies brought their muskets, then the captains may have felt the fifteen Harper's Ferry rifles were all they needed.

The journals are vague about rifles once the expedition started. There are about thirty-five references to rifles, but several of those are references to the same incident by different journalists. The short rifles are referred to directly only during a Columbia River portage and when Lewis is shot. As referred to earlier in this chapter, Lewis's gunshot injury provides us with evidence that the short rifles were of a single caliber. The portage incident of April 12, 1806, took place while the Corps was carrying all its possessions around rapids in the vicinity of the Bridge of the Gods on the Columbia River. Lewis wrote, "we caused all the men who had short rifles to carry them, in order to be prepared for the natives should they make attempts to rob or injure them."[12] This is generally, and reasonably, considered to be evidence that the short rifles were indeed equipped with the slings Lewis requisitioned from military stores at Harper's Ferry. It seems a reasonable conclusion since, had the rifles not had slings, the work force would have been reduced by about half.

During the summer of 1804, when Moses Reed attempted to desert, he "Stold a public Rifle Shot–pouch Powder & Bals."[13] Though "short" is not in the rifle's description, "public" (government issued) would indicate one of the Harper's Ferry rifles. Reed's background is clouded. There are no surviving records that tell whether he came to the Corps of Discovery from the military or from civilian life. He covered his desertion by going back to look for a knife he had "forgotten" at the last camp. Lewis and Clark dispatched a party to hunt him down, and he was returned to the expedition, where he was court martialed, found guilty of desertion, and dishonorably discharged. He continued with the expedition until the following spring, when he was dispatched back down the river with the keelboat.

There is also a hint that, by the spring of 1806, Sergeant Pryor was using a short rifle. In March of that year, Lewis noted that Pryor's rifle was repaired by John Shields and that the rifle was

[12]Moulton, *Journals of the Lewis and Clark Expedition*, 7:112–13.
[13]Ibid., 2:489.

built at Harper's Ferry. Nathaniel Pryor was one of the nine young men from Kentucky. Most researchers think those men would almost certainly have brought their own rifles with them. Does this passage mean that not all did? Does it indicate that he preferred the shorter rifles and had traded firearms for the duration of the trip? Had his weapon been broken beyond John Shields's skills or tools? Or had it been traded to an Indian for some need of the expedition? As the Corps moved east in 1806, John Shields cut off part of the barrels of two rifles that had burst near their muzzles. These were both used in trade with Indians. In particular, one was given to one of their Nez Percé guides. There is no way of telling if these were short rifles or personal ones. One was carried by Richard Windsor, who had come to the Corps from Russell Bissell's company of the 1st Infantry, so he would have joined with a Model 1795 musket. That suggests that one of the damaged weapons was a short rifle. Was the other Pryor's personal rifle? As is often the case, the journals hint and proceed on.

The last hope of finding out what the short rifles were would have been the record of them when they were returned to the army after the expedition. Unfortunately for history, the equipment that returned to St. Louis with the Corps of Discovery was sold as surplus to help defray the trip's expenses. As noted in Donald Jackson's *Letters of the Lewis and Clark Expedition with Related Documents, 1783–1845*, the "Final Summation of Lewis's Account" reads, in part, "being the net proceeds of the sale of Sundry Rifles, Muskets, powder horns, Shot pouches, Powder, Lead, Kettles, Axes, & other public property remaining on hand at the termination of the expedition to the Pacific Ocean, which were disposed of at Public Auction at St. Louis pr. a/c ($)408.62."[14] Thus ends the all-too-short paper trail of the short rifles.

---

[14]Jackson, *Letters of the Lewis and Clark Expedition*, item 277:424.

CHAPTER 4

Personal Weapons

The Frontier was the land of America's dreams, and at the dawn of the nineteenth century it was rapidly becoming the mythological landscape. The frontiersman who would be fixed in literature in another generation by James Fenimore Cooper was already fixed in the American mind by the treatment by popular literature and oral tradition of such men as Daniel Boone. Lewis and Jefferson had talked at length about the type of men who were needed for a trip to the Pacific. When Lewis wrote to Clark to ask him to recruit men for the trip, he was specific that gentlemen were not needed. Lewis and Clark both wanted frontiersmen, men who already knew not just how to hunt but how to make a living by knife and gun, men to whom a roof over their heads was a luxury. Lewis wrote to Clark that he wanted to

> find and engage some good hunters, stout, healthy, unmarried men, accustomed to the woods, and capable of bearing bodily fatigue in a pretty considerable degree; should any young men answering this description be found in your neighborhood I would thank you to give information of them on my arrival at the falls of the Ohio.[1]

The result was the recruiting of the expedition members remembered as the "nine young men from Kentucky": William Bratton, John Colter, the brothers Joseph and Reuben Field, Charles Floyd, George Gibson, Nathaniel Pryor, George Shannon, and John Shields. These nine men were of the Frontier; rifles were normal, everyday tools to them. Knives, large and small, would have been as articles of clothing.

---

[1]Jackson, *Letters of the Lewis and Clark Expedition*, item 46:57.

There is some evidence that the nine brought their own weapons with them. One piece is especially revealing. On August 21, 1804, after Charles Floyd's death, Clark wrote, "& Give Sjt. Pryor Sg Floyds things except shot p[ouch] & Tomhk [tomahawk]."[2] As Charles Floyd's cousin, Nathaniel Pryor was the natural recipient of his possessions. That he was not given the shot pouch and tomahawk could suggest that they were military property. It could as easily mean that he, one of the nine young men, had his own accouterments and that the shot pouch and tomahawk were considered such personal property that the captains intended to return them to Floyd's family. This idea is buttressed by an occurrence during the return leg of the trip.

> This morning Geo. Drewyer accompanied by Hohastillpilp Set out in Serch of two tomahawks of ours which we have understood were in the possession of certain indians resideing at a distance in the Plains on the South Side of Flat Head river, one is a pipe tomahawk which Capt L. left at our Camp on Musquetor Creek and the other was stolen from me whilst we lay at the forks of this and Chopunnish rivers last fall.
>
> *Clark, June 1, 1806[3]*

Lewis finished the story the next day.

> Drewyer arrived this evening with Neeshneparkkeeook and Hohâstillpilp who had accompanyed him to the lodges of the persons who had our tomahawks.   he obtained both the tomahawks principally by the influence of the former of these Cheifs.   the one which had been stolen we prized most as it was the private property of the late Sergt. Floyd and Capt. C. was desireous of returning it to his friends.
>
> *Lewis, June 2, 1806[4]*

The nine young men almost certainly brought rifles with them. We generally assume that every man in Kentucky carried a long rifle, the legendary Kentucky rifle.[5] To some extent that is probably a valid idea. During the late eighteenth and early nineteenth centuries the general term seems to have been "rifle." The government

---

[2]Moulton, *Journals of the Lewis and Clark Expedition*, 2:497.
[3]Ibid., 7:324–25.
[4]Ibid., 7:326.
[5]See note 3 in chapter 3, "Short Rifles."

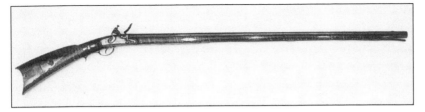

KENTUCKY RIFLE

Also known as "Pennsylvania rifle," from whence the design originated, or "American long rifle." Many of the men who brought personal weapons with them would have had rifles of this type. *Courtesy Buffalo Bill Historical Center, Cody, Wyoming, U.S.A.; Gift of Olin Corporation, Winchester Arms Collection, 1988.8.1040.*

orders for contract rifles during the period sometimes modify the word rifle with adjectives such as "common." According to Norman Flayderman, the term "Kentucky rifle" dates to the period immediately following the War of 1812. The song "The Battle of New Orleans," a.k.a. "The Hunters of Kentucky" (not the one recorded by Johnny Horton in the early 1960s) included the lines:

> But Jackson he was wide awake,
> and wasn't scar'd at trifles,
> for well he knew what aim we take
> with our Kentucky Rifles.

Flayderman goes on to point out that the song's popularity and widespread distribution as a broadsheet seems to be the beginnings of both the name and the legend of the Kentucky rifle.[6] So at the time of the expedition the nine young men were Kentuckians, but their long guns were simply rifles.

Most people today think of the Kentucky rifle as an elegant, often decorated long-barreled gun of relatively small bore, .30 to .36 caliber. A squirrel gun. Yet in the period leading up to the Lewis and Clark Expedition, there were still plenty of bear, some elk, and warfare on the western frontiers. Many folks felt that

---

[6]Flayderman, *Flayderman's Guide to Antique American Firearms*, 659, 660.

slightly larger calibers were called for. While Clark's rifle was, by his own account, small, not all the long rifles of the period were. There are records of .40- to .50-caliber long rifles, but the majority seem to have been .40 caliber or smaller. There is no way of knowing what caliber the nine young men carried, but the type would have fit the image most people have of the Kentucky rifle. The rifles would have been full stocked with octagonal barrels forty to forty-eight inches long. Curly maple was probably the favorite wood for the stocks, certainly the most colorful. The distinctive brass embellishment seen on many surviving long rifles did not become popular, however, until a decade or two later. There were so many good gunsmiths in Pennsylvania producing long rifles that their work became the standard for this first recognized American rifle style.

Besides the soldiers assigned to the Corps of Discovery from the frontier forts and the nine young men from Kentucky, Lewis and Clark recruited boatmen and an interpreter before heading up the Missouri. The interpreter, George Drouillard (usually spelled "Drewyer" by Lewis and Clark), was recruited because of his expertise in sign language, the lingua franca of the West, and his wilderness skills. Lewis met and hired Drouillard at Fort Massac on November 11, 1803, as he approached the mouth of the Ohio. Lewis recognized Drouillard's worth as an interpreter and hired him at $25 a month (far more than the sergeants' $8 a month). He also appreciated Drouillard's wilderness skills during the trip and never went on a long scout away from the main party without him. Drouillard was with Lewis both in the searches for the Shoshones in 1805 and the exploration of the Marias in 1806. Given what we know of his life, none of this is particularly surprising. Drouillard was the son of a French Canadian father and a Shawnee (or maybe Delaware) mother. They had moved to the Cape Girardeau area on the west bank of the Mississippi when he was a child. He grew up as a hunter and trapper, apparently comfortable with both sides of the family. The journals suggest that he was one of the expedition's best hunters and shots. These references, though never mentioning his weapons, hint at his being both well armed and well versed in the use of his weapons.

While the Corps overwintered at Fort Mandan, the captains realized that having another interpreter would serve them well. Drouillard's command of sign language had and would serve the expedition well. But the captains learned from the Mandans that the tribe with whom they would most likely have to trade for horses was Shoshone. There was a trader named Toussaint Charbonneau living in the Mandan villages. Charbonneau didn't speak Shoshone, but the younger of his two wives, Sacagawea, did. She also spoke Hidatsa, as did her husband. Charbonneau didn't speak English, but two of the boatmen recruited in St. Louis, Cruzatte and Labiche, spoke both French and English. A chain of languages is not the best way to translate, but it is far better than not being able to communicate at all. And it is better than sign language, which has its own dialects and accents that can lead to misunderstandings. So the captains hired Charbonneau as a translator and received Sacagawea's services as part of the deal.

Toussaint Charbonneau has a poor reputation with many historians of the expedition. This may be due to the fact that Lewis wrote more about him than Clark did. Lewis strikes one as very much a child of the Revolution. He loved the idea of the United States that Jefferson had done so much to bring about. There seems to have been a certain national chauvinism as a result. Lewis seems to have disliked the French, perhaps because while he was in the army during the 1790s the United States had almost gone to war with France, and he appears to have viewed the Canadians as the same Englishmen we had fought in the Revolution. Charbonneau was French Canadian, and for whatever reason, Lewis's journal entries portray Charbonneau in a bad light in all things save cooking. Clark, on the other hand, seems to have liked the entire family. Not only did he adopt and see to the education of the two Charbonneau children, he saw to Toussaint's employment by the government for most of the rest of his own life.

Many writers, apparently following Lewis's lead, portray Charbonneau as an incompetent. He is described as being afraid of

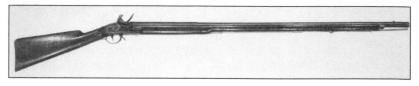

A FUSIL

George Drouillard was described as carrying an elegant fusil. The fusil was the all-purpose, smooth-bored weapon of the frontier. A well-made one such as Drouillard's was accurate enough with a patched ball and could be loaded with bird and buck shot if needed. *Courtesy Michael F. Carrick.*

the water, tipping over a boat on one occasion. His wilderness skills are criticized, in spite of his having lived with Indians, several hundred miles beyond the frontiers of civilization, for years, and to these writers it seems incomprehensible that someone who has lived in the wilderness for such a length of time would not have the skills of Drouillard. But the writers reveal more of their lack of understanding of the West than anything about Charbonneau. The Mandan villages, where he had lived for many years, would have been referred to as a city in the American East—larger than St. Louis or Washington, D.C., and at least as civilized. Charbonneau was not a *coureur de bois* or a *voyageur*—he was a professional interpreter and trader. He was not hired for his wilderness skills but his language skills. In spite of these prejudicial historical assessments, Charbonneau did come prepared for the trip. He brought a teepee big enough not only for his family, but for Lewis, Clark, York, and Drouillard, as well as his own personal gear and likely his own weapon.

By the end of the trip Charbonneau was carrying a government weapon. The one he was likely carrying in 1805 was lost on June 29, 1805, when the Charbonneau family and William Clark were caught in a flash flood in one of the draws running into the Missouri at the Great Falls. As Clark described the incident,

about a 1/4 of a mile above the falls I obsd a Deep rivein [ravine] in which was Shelveing rocks under which we took Shelter near the river

and placed our guns the Compass &c. &c. under a Shelveing rock on
the upper Side of the Creek, in a place which was very secure from
rain, the first Shower was moderate accompanied with a violent wind,
the effects of which we did not feel, Soon after a torrent of rain and
hail fell more violent than ever I Saw before, the rain fell like one voley
of water falling from the heavens and gave us time only to get out of
the way of a torrent of water which was Poreing down the hill in the
rivin with emence force tareing every thing before it takeing with it
large rocks & mud, I took my gun and Shot pouch in my left hand,
and with the right Scrambled up the hill pushing the Interpreters wife
(who had her Child in her arms) before me, the Interpreter himself
makeing attempts to pull up his wife by the hand . . . I lost at the river
in the torrent the large *Compas*, an eligant fusee, Tomahawk, *Hum-
brallo*, Shot pouch, & horn with powder & Ball, mockersons, & the
woman lost her Childs Bear & Clothes bedding &c.

Clark, June 29, 1805[7]

Clark refers both to saving his rifle and shot pouch and to losing
an "elegant fusee" and its accouterments. Clark, who wrote more
about his weapons than any other journalist, never mentions
having more than one rifle, except for this reference. Was this
Clark's or Charbonneau's? If Clark's, had he lent it to Charbonneau for the trip? The compass and umbrella were clearly
Clark's from other references. The "Childs Bear" was the child's,
Baptiste's, cradle board. The tomahawk could have been Clark's,
though he refers to having a personal one later. So the gun and
tomahawk could have well been Charbonneau's. The important
point is that Charbonneau's concern was with the safety of his
wife and child, not the equipment.

The fusil was a short musket. The word is French, as was the
origin of the weapon. The French had developed it as an alternative to the heavier military musket, and it was issued to special
troops. Fusils were usually smooth bored but were occasion-
ally rifled. The design became popular with civilians as well,
especially along and beyond France's North American frontiers.
The word "fusil" is derived from *foisil*, the steel used for striking
sparks in fire starting. The English corrupted the pronunciation

---

[7]Moulton, *Journals of the Lewis and Clark Expedition*, 4:342–43.

into "fusee" or "fuzee." In America the term came to be applied
to trade muskets. Since those weapons were generally not top
quality, Clark's use of the adjective "elegant" indicates that the
piece was not a trade musket but a well-made, short-barreled
personal weapon. Whether it was Clark's or Charbonneau's, it
was lost, and after that Charbonneau would have carried one of
the expedition weapons when he was walking ashore.

As mentioned, William Clark wrote more about his personal
rifle than did any other journalist. But he did not write much.
On August 8, 1804, Clark wrote, "I took one man and went on
Shore the man Killed and Elk   I fired 4 times at one & did
not Kill him, my ball being Small I think was the reason."[8] Again
on October 2, 1804, Clark makes a somewhat cryptic note: "Little
gun all my hunting."[9] This seems to indicate that he used his one
small-caliber rifle most if not all the time. Does this mean he
was not using his short, elegant fusil, or that he was not using
a Harper's Ferry short rifle? Since the expedition's hunters were
keeping the Corps well fed at that time, one can perhaps speculate
that either some men had larger-caliber weapons or that they were
using the larger-caliber short rifles. The day before Lewis had
written that Pierre Cruzatte had wounded both a grizzly bear and
a buffalo but had been forced to flee from both of them. Lewis
states that Cruzatte was using a short rifle twenty-two months
later when he accidentally shot Lewis. Was Cruzatte using the
short rifle in October 1804, or some other weapon? And were the
woundings of the bear and buffalo due to an inadequate weapon,
or to Cruzatte's poor aim because of his nearsightedness? Too,
over those months had there been a discussion about the rela-
tive merits of the various weapons in dealing with the large and
dangerous animals they were hunting in the West? Or was Clark
idly speculating on the topic in the summer of 1804?

It has been suggested that Clark's references to his Small rifle
means he was carrying a rifle made by John N. Small, a region-
ally prominent gunsmith whom Clark could have known. John

_____

[8]Ibid., 2:459.
[9]Ibid., 3:189.

Small was born sometime in the middle of the eighteenth century. By 1775 he was working as a gunsmith in West Augusta, Virginia, and by 1788 he had relocated to the Western frontier and was working as a gunsmith between New Lisbon, Columbiana County, Ohio, and Vincennes, Knox County, Indiana.[10] Since Columbiana County is in eastern Ohio and Vincennes, Indiana is on the Wabash River, the search for him can be narrowed to two states. William Clark served with Gen. Anthony Wayne in the Northwest campaigns of the 1790s and could have met and purchased a rifle from John Small at that time. The journal entry that leads to the speculation was made on December 9, 1805, near the Columbia River, when Clark wrote, "a flock of Brant lit in the Creek which was 70 yds wide I took up my Small rifle and Shot one which astonished those people verry much."[11] The fact that he unnecessarily capitalized two other words in the entry and the reference to his "Small ball" in the preceding paragraph here more strongly points to his references being to a small-caliber rifle, not a manufacturer's name.

Clark's rifle was apparently a good weapon, and he certainly liked it. There is some evidence that he had used the rifle a long time and shot quite a bit. On the return trip, April 7, 1806, he wrote, "We made our men exersise themselves in Shooting and regulateing their guns, found Several of them that had their Sights moved by accident, and others that wanted Some little alterations all which were compleated rectified in the Course of the day except my Small rifle, which I found wanted Cutting out."[12] The next day he wrote that "John Shields Cut out my Small rifle & brought hir to Shoot very well."[13] The significance of these two entries, other than what it shows of Shields's ability, is to illustrate the condition of Clark's rifle. "Cutting out" refers to deepening the rifling grooves. Every time a rifle is fired, even though the steel barrel is much harder than the soft lead of the bullet, there is a slight amount of wear on it. For that wear to be

[10]Whisker, *Arms Makers of Pennsylvania*, 176.
[11]Moulton, *Journals of the Lewis and Clark Expedition*, 6:119.
[12]Ibid., 7:92.
[13]Ibid., 7:95.

significant enough to require the grooves to be deepened means that Clark had fired thousands of rounds through the rifle.

There is another instance of Clark speaking favorably of his rifle even when it failed him. While starving during the Bitterroot Mountains crossing, he wrote on September 16, 1805, "I saw 4 Black tail Deer to day before we Set out which came up the mountain and what is Singular Snaped 7 tims at a large buck.   it is Singular as my gun has a Steel frisen and never Snaped 7 times before   in examining her found the flint loose."[14] To "snap" means that he cocked the hammer and pulled the trigger, but the hammer's fall against the frizzen either failed to throw sparks or the sparks failed to ignite the powder in the pan. If the leather padding between the flint and hammer vise had gotten wet from the snowy weather, it is possible that it wouldn't have held the flint tightly enough. Or perhaps Clark had somehow rubbed or struck the vise's screw and slightly loosened the device (for a more complete explanation, see appendix B). Even with such problems, Clark sounds like a man who trusted his rifle and would prefer being careful with his aim to switching to a larger-caliber rifle that did not feel comfortable. This is not an uncommon issue with riflemen. Though most outfitters I know discourage hunters from using .270s for elk hunting on the theory that the cartridge is too light for a seven hundred–pound animal, many continue to do so. The fact is that the only time Clark complained of his rifle being too small is the one time mentioned here. Perhaps he decided to be sure of his shots after that and was a good enough shot to do so successfully.

It is possible that Clark also had a pistol of his own. There is no reference to any except for his trading one for a horse on August 29, 1805: "I purchased a horse for which I gave my Pistol 100 Balls Powder & a Knife." The possessive may have indicated a personal weapon, though he did not apply for recompense from the government for it. The possessive could as easily referred to one of the horse pistols Lewis requisitioned at Harper's Ferry.

---

[14]Ibid., 5:209.

York probably had a rifle of his own. There is a single piece of evidence in the journals to support this supposition:

> Last night we were all allarmed by a large buffaloe Bull, which swam over from the opposite shore and coming along side of the white perogue, climbed over it to land, he then alarmed ran up the bank in full speed directly towards the fires, and was within 18 inches of the heads of some of the men who lay sleeping before the centinel could allarm him or make him change his course, still more alarmed, he now took his direction immediately towards our lodge, passing between 4 fires and within a few inches of the heads of one range of men as they yet lay sleeping, when he came near the tent, my dog saved us by caus-ing him to change his course a second time, which he did by turning a little to the right, and was quickly out of sight, leaving us by this time all in an uproar with our guns in our hands, enquiring of each other the case of the alarm, which after a few moments was explained by the cen-tinel; we were happy to find no one hirt. The next morning we found that the buffaloe in passing the perogue had trodden on a rifle, which belonged to Capt. Clark's black man, who had negligently left her in the perogue, the rifle is much bent, he had also broken the spindle, pivot, and shattered the stock of one of the bluntderbushes on board, with this damage I felt well content, happey indeed, that we had sus-tained no further injury.   it appears that the white perogue, which contains our most valuable stores, is attended by some evil gennii.
>
> *Lewis, May 29, 1805*[15]

In York's defense, Clark does not hold the rifle's damage against him, and Lewis fails to explain why leaving a rifle in the pirogue was neglectful, but leaving a blunderbuss there was not. While escaping without injury was the best news, there was further good news. Apparently John Shields was able to repair the dam-ages when he set up his forge for the last time at the mouth of the Marias River. Both blunderbusses are listed as functional after they are picked up from the cache at Great Falls on the return trip. It is, of course, possible that the damaged blunderbuss's swivel did not work and it could only be shoulder fired. It seems likely that York's rifle is one of the ones referred to later in the journals as having had the barrel sawed off.

---

[15]Ibid., 4:215.

Since York was a slave, his being armed might seem strange to some. But he and Clark had been constant companions since childhood. Almost certainly they had hunted together all their lives. It would have been natural for York to have been armed on the frontier, and he would likely have been a competent hunter and woodsman. Not until a generation or so later, when the southern wilderness had been subdued, did anyone in the South give any thought to the advisability of keeping slaves unarmed.

Meriwether Lewis brought at least seventeen military weapons with him from Harper's Ferry; fifteen short rifles and two horse pistols. He also brought a number of personal weapons. While he was in Philadelphia, he purchased two cased pocket pistols from Robert Barnhill.[16] Lewis did trade off one of his personal pistols and some ammunition for a horse, indicating how much more important horses were than pistols. Lewis also carried his personal long rifle. Unlike Clark, Lewis never wrote about the caliber of his weapon. He certainly felt well armed with it:

> I walked on shore this morning for the benefit of exersice which I much wanted, and also to examine the country and it's productions, in these excurtions I most generally went alone armed with my rifle and espontoon: thus equiped I feel myself more than an equal match for a brown bear provided I get him in open woods or near the water but I feel myself a little diffident with respect to an attack in the open plains, I have therefore come to the resolution to act on the defencive only, should I meet these gentlemen [grizzlies] in the open country.
>
> *Lewis, May 12, 1805*[17]

The above passage may indicate that Lewis had given thought to dealing with grizzlies. That is not surprising, since the Corps had already had a few close calls with the big bears. It was just over a month later that Lewis had an encounter he had not relished.

> I selected a fat buffaloe and shot him very well, through the lungs; while I was gazeing attentively on the poor anamal discharging blood in streams from his mouth and nostrils, expecting him to fall every instant, and having entirely forgotton to reload my rifle, a large white, or reather brown bear, had perceived and crept on me within 20 steps

---

[16]Jackson, *Letters of the Lewis and Clark Expedition*, item 55:91.
[17]Moulton, *Journals of the Lewis and Clark Expedition*, 4:145.

before I discovered him; in the first moment I drew up my gun to shoot, but at the same instant recolected that she was not loaded and that he was too near for me to hope to perform this opperation before he reached me, as he was then briskly advancing on me; it was an open level plain, not a bush within miles nor a tree within less than three hundred yards of me; the river bank was sloping and not more than three feet above the level of the water; in short there was no place by means of which I could conceal myself from this monster untill I could charge my rifle; in this situation I thought of retreating in a brisk walk as fast as he was advancing untill I could reach a tree about three hundred yards below me, but I had no sooner terned myself about but he pitched at me, opened mouthed and full speed,[18] I ran about 80 yards and found he gained on me fast, I then run into the water   the idea struk me to get into the water to such a debth that I could stand and he would be obliged to swim, and that I could in that situation defend myself with my espontoon; accordingly I ran haistily into the water about waist deep, and faced about and presented the point of my espontoon, at this instant he arrived at the edge of the water within about 20 feet of me; the moment I put myself in this attitude of defence he sudonly wheeled about as if frightened, declined the combat on such unequal grounds, and retreated with quite as great precipitation as he had justbefore pursued me. . . . My gun reloaded I felt confidence once more in my strength; and determined not to be thwarted in my design of visiting medicine river, but determined never again to suffer my peice to be longer empty than the time she necessarily required too charge her.

Lewis, June 14, 1805[19]

Lewis may have been fortunate to have forgotten to reload on that occasion. Unless he was very lucky shooting a grizzly at twenty steps with a long rifle, he certainly would have been in dire straits even if his shot was not instantly fatal.

Few writers have mentioned that Lewis had a personal shotgun with him. Lewis was collecting birds and small mammals for scientific examination during the trip, and a shotgun was the ideal weapon for such work. But Lewis never mentions having a shotgun. There are few references as to how specimen animals

---

[18]Probably not full speed. An Olympic-class sprinter can, out of the blocks on a good track, run about 33 feet per second. An old, fat grizzly can cover about 44 feet per second through the sagebrush. Personal notes, timed off film.

[19]Moulton, *Journals of the Lewis and Clark Expedition*, 4:292–93.

A FOWLING PIECE

Today we would call it a shotgun. It was long barreled, smooth bored, and designed to fire birdshot. Lewis had some type of fowling piece, and since he never commented on it in the journals, it was probably plain, somewhat like this one. *Courtesy Michael F. Carrick.*

were collected. But the "Final Summation of Lewis' Account" records the following:

> For one Uniform Laced Coat, one silver Epaulet, one Dirk & belt, one hanger & belt, one pistol & one fowling piece, all private property, given in exchange for Canoe, Horses &c. for public service during the expedition & admitted to his credit by order of the Secretary of War.   135.00[20]

Since that is the sole reference, there is no way of knowing what the weapon looked like, how much it was used, and when it was traded for what.

As officers, Lewis and Clark would have personal swords, and at least Lewis had an espontoon. They will be discussed in the chapter on edged weapons. Lewis had an air rifle, but it has its own story and hence its own chapter.

There is no record of what types of weapons the engagés carried. It seems reasonable to assume that men who were accustomed to life on the big rivers of the West were men who carried weapons, but there is no clear reference to what, if any, weapons these men carried. Clark, on May 18, 1804, indicated that he gave knives to three of the "French hands," suggesting that at least some of the men were short of some needed items.

The expedition's success indicates that the captains recruited well. The weapons brought by the men who joined seem to have been adequate to the needs of the trip.

---

[20]Jackson, *Letters of the Lewis and Clark Expedition,* item 277:428.

CHAPTER 5

Pistols

The weapon most associated with the American West is the six-shooter. But Samuel Colt wasn't born until 1814, eight years after Lewis and Clark returned. At the beginning of the nineteenth century, pistols were still gentlemen's weapons. The captains both wrote of carrying pistols and of trading them for horses. There is no evidence that anyone on the expedition fired a pistol. Clark did write of loading a brace of them on one occasion when he anticipated trouble, and Lewis did draw one during the fight with the Blackfeet. The records indicate that Lewis had four pistols when he left Pittsburgh, and it is possible that other men owned and carried pistols. Clark, for instance, may well have had a personal pistol, since he was an officer and a gentleman. Though Clark did refer to trading one of his pistols, he did not ask for reimbursement for a personal pistol as Lewis did after the expedition. It is easy to imagine that Clark carried one of the two military-issue pistols Lewis brought from Harper's Ferry. Lewis had also purchased two pocket pistols in Philadelphia. There is no direct evidence of more than those four pistols in the Corps of Discovery.

Horseman's pistols were big, designed to be carried in holsters mounted on either side of a saddle's pommel. Pocket pistols were smaller, meant to be carried, as the name implies, in one's pocket. Not all were derringer-sized, though. While there were pistols small enough to carry in a vest pocket, the long coats of the day often had sizable pockets built just for pistols. For instance, the forked tails of a frock coat lent themselves to pistol pockets.

So, while Lewis's may not have been small enough for a vest pocket, they would have been smaller and of smaller bore than the horse pistols.

All we can know for sure about the two horseman's pistols is that the purveyor of military stores acquired, for Captain Lewis, "1 pr. Horsemans Pistols."[1] There are three possibilities of what that brace of pistols were.

Robert M. Reilly's *United States Martial Flintlocks* states that the government had 320 Model 1797 Horseman's Pistols assembled under contract, with uniform parts purchased overseas. There were three contractors: Thomas Annely, who made 22; Robert McCormick, who made 98; and John Miles, who made 200. There is no clear reference of how many, if any, of these were stored at Harper's Ferry. While each builder's pistols were uniform, there was no uniformity throughout the contract. So, while all of them looked similar—a full-length stock with ramrod under the smooth-bored barrel and large, deep butt cap—they had marked differences. McCormick's varied in length from 15¼ to 16¼ inches long, weighed around 2½ pounds and were .67 caliber. Miles's were about the same length and weight, but were .60 caliber. Annely apparently did not place an identifying mark on the pistols he made. There are a few surviving examples that are unmarked, and these may well be Annely's. If so, he made pistols that about 16 inches long, 2½ pounds, and .67 caliber.[2]

The second possibility is the Model 1799, often referred to as the North & Cheney model.

These were the first military pistols made in the United States without foreign parts. According to Arcadi Gluckman's *U.S. Martial Pistols and Revolvers*, in 1798 Congress appropriated $800,000 "for the purchase of arms and ammunition to augment the output of the Springfield Armory." Contracts were then awarded to private firms. Simeon North of Berlin, Connecticut, received a contract for 500 pistols in 1799. These were

[1]Jackson, *Letters of the Lewis and Clark Expedition*, item 57:98.
[2]Reilly, *United States Martial Flintlocks*, 164–67.

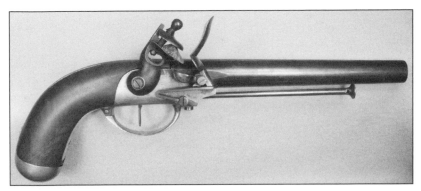

A REPLICA NORTH & CHENEY PISTOL
This is a copy of the most likely type of pistol Lewis procured at the Harper's Ferry Arsenal. *Courtesy Michael F. Carrick.*

so satisfactory that 1,500 more were ordered in 1800. Though the North family history indicates that Elisha Cheney was never a true partner in the firm, the pistols were marked NORTH & CHENEY, BERLIN. The two men were brothers-in-law, and however their business arrangement worked, the firm delivered 2,000 pistols by the fall of 1802, modeled, as the contract specified, after the French Model 1777. There were some modifications, mainly lengthening the barrel by one inch and changing the bore to the same as the Model 1795 musket's .69 caliber. The result was a very practical and useful pistol, though it is not as pleasing to the eye as most pistols of the period, since it has no forearm. The ramrod slides into the frame on the lower right side, sticking out beside, but not touching, the barrel. The pistols were about 14½ inches long and weighed about 3¼ pounds.[3]

The third possibility is that Lewis received some of the older pistols listed in the military inventory. These pistols could have been anything left from as far back as the Revolution. There is no record of what, if any, older pistols were at Harper's Ferry.

---

[3]Gluckman, *U.S. Martial Pistols & Revolvers*, 36.

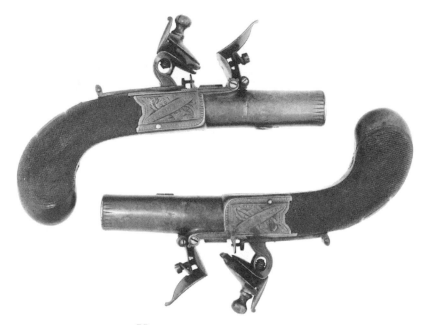

HIDDEN TRIGGER PISTOLS

Something similar to this set of pistols is what most experts feel Lewis purchased in Philadelphia. The trigger drops down when the pistol is cocked. *Courtesy Michael F. Carrick.*

Lewis had carte blanche at Harper's Ferry. It is likely that he received the pistols he asked for. That would mean either Model 1797s or Model 1799s. The Model 1799 would seem to be the likeliest choice, since they were the newest and probably thought of as the best in the inventory. Too, they fired the same size ball as the Model 1795 Muskets. But at that time Lewis was still planning for a party of only fifteen, and since he was receiving the short rifles, the matching caliber advantage may not have mattered.

While he was in Philadelphia, Lewis purchased a pair of pistols, for which there is limited information. Donald Jackson's *Letters of the Lewis and Clark Expedition with Related Documents, 1783–1845,* under "Supplies from Private Venders," states that

Lewis purchased "1 Pair Pocket Pistols, Secret Triggers $10." This transaction was with Robert Barnhill, a storekeeper at 63 North 2nd Street.[4] A secret trigger is one that folds into the frame until the hammer is cocked. The guns' price and Lewis's attraction to them suggests that they were not plain pistols, but a cased set of elegant, refined weapons with all accouterments. They may not have been perfectly suited for the expedition, but they made a good trade item.

On April 29, 1806, Lewis wrote, "we gave small medals to two inferior cheifs of this nation and they each presented us a fine horse in return we gave them sundry articles and among others one of my case pistols and several hundred rounds of ammunition."[5] By the spring of 1806 the Corps of Discovery needed horses much more than pistols or swords; Clark had traded his sword the day before.

A letter dated January 10, 1810, from I. A. Coles about Lewis's effects includes the following:

In the large Trunk a Pistol case—containing a Pocket Pistol—3 Knives &c. &c.
8 Tin Canisters containing a variety of small articles of little value.
A Sword, Tomahawk, Pike blade & part of the Handle[6]

Had this pistol case, pistol, one or more of the knives, the sword, tomahawk, and pike (espontoon) crossed the continent? And where did they end up?

On August 29, 1805, Clark wrote, "I purchased a horse for which I gave my Pistol 100 Balls Powder & a Knife."[7] At this point the Corps was desperate for horses. The next day Clark gave his "Fuzee" to one of the men and then sold the man's musket for the last horse they needed to make it over the mountains. Clark had recorded losing his fuzee two months earlier in a flash

[4]Jackson, *Letters of the Lewis and Clark Expedition*, item 55:91.
[5]Moulton, *Journals of the Lewis and Clark Expedition*, 7:183.
[6]Jackson, *Letters of the Lewis and Clark Expedition*, item 303:472. It seems likely that the sword, tomahawk, espontoon, pistol, and maybe even a knife or two had been to the Pacific with Lewis.
[7]Moulton, *Journals of the Lewis and Clark Expedition*, 5:178.

flood at Great Falls. Was he using "fuzee" to describe any small rifle? Was he using "fuzee" to describe the short rifles? Were there more guns than the records indicate?

For the most part, Lewis's and Clark's pistols seemed to have been most useful as trade items. But twice the officers found they were at least strong psychological support. On March 30, 1804, Clark apparently wrote that he loaded "a small pr Pistols."[8] (The text is difficult to read since it both falls in a crease in the page and was lined through.) This was either because he and Lewis anticipated trouble over their announcing the verdict of the court martial, held the day before, of John Shields, John Colter, and Robert Frazer, or that they were worried about someone trying to steal goods from the supplies due to be delivered that day, or both. For whatever reason, the guns were not needed. In his edition of the *Journals of the Lewis and Clark Expedition*, Gary Moulton speculates that "Clark may have crossed the passage out after the trouble failed to materialize."[9]

Over two years later, in the summer of 1806, Lewis drew one of the pistols in his engagement with the Blackfeet. On the night of July 26, 1806, Lewis and three men who had been searching for the headwaters of the Marias camped with a group of eight young Blackfeet who were returning from a horse raid. They had camped together largely because neither side trusted the other out of its sight. The affair the next morning is well known, and Lewis's pistol played a major part in the story.

Lewis was awakened by a shout.

> I jumped up and asked what was the matter which I quickly learned when I saw drewyer in a scuffle with the indian for his gun.   I reached to seize my gun but found her gone,   I then drew a pistol from my holster and terning myself about saw the indian making off with my gun   I ran at him with my pistol and bid him lay down my gun [at that instant]   which he was in the act of doing when the Fieldses returned and drew up their guns to shoot him which I forbid as he did not appear to be about to make any resistance or commit any

---

[8] Ibid., 2:183.
[9] Ibid., 2:183, n. 1.

offensive act, he dropped the gun and walked slowly off, I picked her
up instantly. . . . pursued the man who had taken my gun who with
another was driving off a part of the horses which were to the left of
the camp, I pursued them so closely that they could not take twelve
of their own horses but continued to drive one of mine with some
others; at the distance of three hundred paces they entered one of
those steep niches in the bluff with the horses before them   being
nearly out of breath I could pursue no farther.   I called to them
as I had done several times before that I would shoot them if they
did not give me my horse and raised my gun, one of them jumped
behind a rock and spoke to the other who turned   arround and
stoped at the distance of 30 steps from me and I shot him through
the belly, he fell to his knees and on his wright elbow from which
position he partly   raised himself up and fired at me, and turning
himself about crawled in behind a rock which was a few feet from
him.   he overshot me, being bearheaded I felt the wind of his bullet very distinctly.   not having my shot pouch I could not reload
my   peice and as there were two of them behind good shelters
from me I did not think it prudent to rush on them with my pistol
which had I discharged I had not the means of reloading untill I
reached camp;

Lewis, July 27, 1806[10]

So Lewis's pistol both prevented one man from stealing his rifle
and allowed Lewis to make a strategic withdrawal after shooting
one of the men who was trying to drive off a horse.

One shouldn't get the idea that pistols were viewed unfavor-
ably in the West. At the beginning of the nineteenth century
any firearm had value. Obviously, Indians were willing to trade
for pistols as well as muskets or rifles. By the time the Corps of
Discovery had reached the mouth of the Willamette River in
November 1805, it was beginning to find Indians armed with
pistols as well as clothing and other goods that most certainly
came from mariners trading around the mouth of the Columbia.

Soon after Several Canoes of Indians from the village above came
down dressed for the purpose as I Supposed of Paying us a friendly
visit, they had Scarlet & blue blankets Salors jackets, overalls, Shirts
and Hats independent of their Usial dress; the most of them had

---

[10]Ibid., 8:134–35.

either war axes Spears or Bows sprung with quivers of arrows, Muskets or pistols, and tin flasks to hold their powder;

Clark, November 4, 1805[11]

All in all, a well-dressed, well-armed group. One that speaks volumes about the coastal trade at the beginning of the nineteenth century.

There is no mention of the types of pistols Clark saw. One might expect these to be ship's pistols, since the Indians had obtained them in trade with sailors. By 1805 the coastal trade was well developed. Over a dozen ships had plied the Northwest coast that fall before the expedition arrived at the mouth of the Columbia. As Lewis and Clark noted, the coastal tribes were much more sophisticated traders than the expedition had become accustomed to. The trade was well developed and goods were already being manufactured solely for that trade. The tribes were very specific about what they would and would not accept. Pistols tended to be a secondary item; muskets were the preferred firearm. The result was a more or less standardized type of trade musket in the Pacific Northwest. There are no such references to a standardized trade pistol. That suggests that any pistols available at the right price were being secured for trade.

Two generations after the expedition, the pistol would become an inseparable piece of the myth of the American West. But in the first decade of the nineteenth century, Lewis and Clark rightly felt the horse to be much more important. Indeed, while their pistols were useful, their horses were critical. The captains recognized that and willingly traded pistols for horses. Yet Lewis seemingly kept one of those secret trigger pistols. When it was inventoried after his death, was it loaded with anything other than memories?

---

[11]Ibid., 6:17.

CHAPTER 6

Air Rifle

T he image that leaps to mind for most people when they hear the term "air rifle" is a Daisy BB gun, which leads to thinking that Meriwether Lewis had brought a toy along to impress the Indians. It did impress the Indians, but not as a toy. At the beginning of the nineteenth century there were many people who were not happy with gunpowder and the firearms it produced. These were not antigun people. They were gun designers and manufacturers who were displeased with many of the characteristics of gunpowder, such as cost, the fouling problems associated with dirty burning, the fact that powder often varied from batch to batch, and the fact that it might not work at all in wet or even damp weather. Then there was the fact that gunpowder produced so much smoke when a weapon was fired that the shooter's vision was often obscured too much to see whether he had hit his mark. Some of these people thought compressed air offered a viable alternative.

As the eighteenth century gave way to the nineteenth, there were many gunsmiths in Europe producing compressed air weapons powerful enough to use for big game hunting or as military weapons. Air rifles had a number of advantages. Though not silent, they were much quieter than firearms. The noise they produced was a low-frequency pop that was hard to recognize or to pinpoint if one couldn't see the shooter. And compressed air doesn't smoke when an air gun is fired. Armies of the day fought at close range with massed troops. After the first couple of volleys the field was so obscured that aiming was difficult at best.

A musket had to be reloaded—powder, ball, and priming—for each shot. That added up to about four shots a minute. An air rifle with 750 pounds-per-square-inch of air pressure in its air cylinder could be discharged twenty to forty times before losing power.

It did take some time and effort to pump up a cylinder. With a hand pump, up to 1,500 strokes might be required to fully charge a cylinder; not a problem for a hunter, but potentially a problem for a soldier. Armies solved this problem by using larger multicylinder cart pumps and by supplying air riflemen with several air cylinders. The Austrian army equipped its air rifle companies with enough air cylinders and balls for four to five hundred shots per soldier, this at a time when most armies issued twenty to a hundred rounds per man.[1]

Why didn't armies convert from firearms to air rifles? Some accounts point to the Napoleonic Wars between 1796 and 1815. The French, so the stories go, didn't have the manufacturing technology to produce air rifles. Napoleon, on the other hand, was facing Austrian troops armed with high-quality repeating air rifles. These troops had a much higher rate of fire, and sans smoke it was more accurate. There are stories that Napoleon had captured air riflemen shot as terrorists, making it hard to recruit men for the air rifle companies. Research and development therefore slowed, and the weapons became very exclusive, expensive, and therefore limited in manufacture and in use. In the meantime, firearm technology improved throughout the nineteenth century, ending with the metallic cartridge and smokeless powder. So the firearm won the competition.

There is some evidence to support the above-mentioned stories. In 1802, during a lull in the Napoleonic Wars, Col. Thomas Thornton traveled in France and spent some time with Gen. Edouard Mortier, the future *maréchal* of France. Thornton wrote:

> One day in particular, General Mortier, in speaking of air guns, recalled to the recollection of some officers in the company a circumstance which happened after the retreat of the enemy, but where I cannot precisely call to mind. He said, "do you remember when I

---

[1]Wolff, *Air Guns,* 29.

had ordered the cannon to cease firing that an orderly sergeant who was standing close to us leaped up very high into the air and then fell down? We supposed, at first, that he was in a fit, and we were greatly astonished to find him dead, as nothing had been heard to injure him. On his being undressed, however, a ball was found to have struck him, which must have been shot from an air-gun in the adjoining field and aimed at us." "Yes," replied one of the officers, "I remember it well, and I think we had a fortunate escape." They then stated, that on account of this treachery they hung all of that corps that fell into their hands, considering them not as soldiers but as assassins, and never after gave any quarter. They acknowledged, at the same time, that they lost many fine men by that corps of Austrians, which they stated consist of about five hundred men.[2]

Thornton's book may well be the origin of the tales of the Austrians' inability to recruit or keep men in air rifle companies, resulting in the guns going out of service. Some other sources, in particular Fred Baer, point to the delicacy of air rifle mechanisms and the difficulty of building air cylinders that could stand up to the high pressures needed as more likely reasons for most armies not using them. The Austrians did use repeating air rifles against both the Turks and the French, but Baer indicates only the numbers used, the trouble the army had acquiring enough air cylinders, apparently due to the difficulty of constructing reliable ones, and their final resting places in magazines and arsenals as troops were equipped with flintlocks.[3]

W. H. B. Smith, who quotes Thornton extensively, goes on to state that a Hauptman Halla wrote in 1890:

> The fact that this remarkable weapon nevertheless did not remain in use and was removed as expendable supply to the fortress of Olmutz in 1815 was due not only to the changed tactical principles, but chiefly to the circumstance that there were no adequately trained riflesmiths available to take care of the delicate component parts of the locks and valves, and therefore the percentage of unusable air rifles shown in the reports was frighteningly high.[4]

[2]From Thomas Thornton, *A Sporting Tour Through France in the Year 1802*, 2:59. Quoted in Smith's *Gas, Air and Spring Guns of the World*, 25.

[3]Fred Barer, "Napoleon Was Not Afraid of It," in Held, *Arms and Armor Annual*, 1:250.

[4][first name not given] Halla, *Bulletins of the Military Archives for the Year 1890*. Quoted in Smith, *Gas, Air and Spring Guns of the World*, 30.

This would suggest that the air rifles were considered good and viable weapons and not retired from service until they had been in use for twenty-five years. There is the added fact that in 1815 the Napoleonic Wars ended at Waterloo and the Austrian army was in a position to give up some of its arms as part of the army was discharged. Smith goes on to write:

> The Austrians treated the development as a real secret weapon. A special shop was set up for Girandoni and workers were specially selected and sworn to secrecy about equivalent to that required for an H-Bomb "Q" clearance today.
>
> It should be mentioned in passing that the Girandoni pattern was produced by other makers on contract. Then, even as now, Austria was a hotbed of small gunmakers who were good at duplication.[5]

Smith seems to contradict himself in the above paragraphs. Austria wasn't going to keep a weapon secret by giving the design to a number of different manufacturing firms, most of which were in foreign countries. The Girandoni design was consciously spread to various German principalities and to Switzerland and England by the Austrian government. That strongly suggests that there was no attempt to keep the weapon secret. From any of those countries the design and quite possibly a weapon itself could easily have found its way to the United States.

The Girandoni air rifles represented a technology that teased generals and sportsmen alike. Lewis was one of the teased. For an expedition such as the one on which he was embarking, an air rifle such as a Girandoni would serve well as a way to impress the various tribes with the power of the United States. A rifle that needed no gunpowder was likely to impress tribes who had to trade for expensive and scarce gunpowder. And the weapon could serve as a backup if the Corps lost its gunpowder. So Meriwether Lewis, somehow, somewhere, acquired one.

Lewis's air rifle enters the Expedition journals on the day Lewis began recording the journey.

> went on shore and being invited on by some of the gentlemen present to try my *airgun* which I purchased   brought it on shore charged it

---

[5]Smith, *Gas, Air and Spring Guns of the World*, 30.

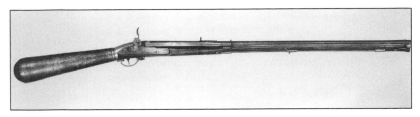

GIRANDONI AIR RIFLE (RIGHT SIDE VIEW)

Notice that there is no frizzen and pan in front of the hammer. The hammer sets the air charge for the trigger to release; there is no need for spark of fire. Also note that the butt stock is metal; it is the air cylinder for the weapon, holding air compressed to about 750 psi. *Courtesy Michael F. Carrick.*

GIRANDONI AIR RIFLE (RIGHT SIDE CLOSE-UP)

This view shows the metal butt stock and the tubal magazine in front of the hammer more clearly. *Courtesy Michael F. Carrick.*

GIRANDONI AIR RIFLE (TOP VIEW)

In this view one can see the magazine tube on the right, in front of the hammer. The breech block sticks out on the left. *Courtesy Michael F. Carrick.*

and fired myself seven times fifty five yards with pretty good success; after which a Mr. Blaze Cenas being unacquainted with the management of the gun suffered her to discharge herself accidently   the ball passed through the hat of a woman about 40 yards distanc cuting her temple about the fourth of the diameter of the ball; shee feel instantly and the blood gusing from her temple   we were all in the greatest consternation   supposed she was dead by [but] in a minute she revived to our enespressable satisfaction, and by examination we found the wound by no means mortal or even dangerous.

Lewis, August 30, 1803[6]

There is an obvious question. How did Lewis find a man west of Pittsburgh who was "unacquainted with the management of the gun?" In 1803, guns were a part of life that far west. One possible answer is that Lewis's air gun was somehow different from the guns to which men along the Ohio River were accustomed. The Corps of Discovery's journals aren't much help. The next time the air gun is mentioned is almost a year later, when, on August 3, 1804, an entry makes a typical allusion to the air gun, saying simply that Lewis had fired it "a few times" for the Otos with whom they were visiting.

On his way down the Ohio, Lewis wrote that he spent some time with Col. Thomas Rodney, on his way from Delaware to the lower Mississippi. On September 8, 1803, Rodney wrote a bit more about the meeting:

> Visited Captain Lewess barge. He shewed us his air gun which fired 22 times at one charge. He shewed us the mode of charging her and then loaded with 12 balls which he intended to fire one at a time; but she by some means lost the whole charge of air at the first fire. He charged her again and then she fired twice. He then found the cause and in some measure prevented the airs escaping, and then she fired seven times; but when in perfect order she fires 22 times in a minute. All the balls are put at once into a short side barrel and are then droped into the chamber of the gun one at a time by moving a spring; and when the triger is pulled just so much air escapes out of the bag which forms the britch [breech] of the gun serves for one ball. It is a curious piece of workmanship not easily discribed and therefore I omit attempting it.[7]

---

[6]Moulton, *Journals of the Lewis and Clark Expedition*, 2:65.
[7]Rodney, *A Journey through the West*, 50, 62.

This helps to visualize Lewis's air rifle but also presents a problem. It contradicts all we knew about that particular air gun before Michael Carrick published the above passage in "Meriwether Lewis's Air Gun," his paper on Rodney's description of Lewis's air gun, in 2002. Will Rogers once said that it wasn't what we don't know that gets us in trouble, "it's all the things we know that just ain't so." For the last quarter century, historians looking into Lewis's air gun have all fallen into the trap of circular reasoning.[8]

The loop of misunderstanding began in 1977, when Henry M. Stewart, Jr., published a paper revealing that he'd found, in Isaiah Lukens's estate papers, evidence of the disposition of Lewis's air rifle. Lukens, a Philadelphia clockmaker and gunsmith, died in 1846. In January of 1847 his estate was auctioned off. Item 95 in the auction catalogue states: "1 large do [air gun] made for and used by Messrs Lewis & Clark in their exploring expedition. A *great curiosity.*"[9]

There is no record of who purchased item 95, so the trail turns cold from there and the circular reasoning begins.

Lukens, perhaps best known in his own day as a clock maker (he made the clock for the tower of Independence Hall), was also a maker of air guns. He had perfected a valve for air guns that solved their greatest problem, decreased air pressure after each shot. His guns were considered some of the finest of the period. And he moved in the same Philadelphia circles Lewis was moving in during the spring and summer of 1803. So, the logic said, since Lukens had the air gun in 1846 and since the estate sale said it was "made for" Lewis and Clark, it must have been one of his that Lewis had bought and either returned to him after the expedition or that Lukens reacquired after Lewis's death. Suddenly, the older question of what the air gun was seemed to be solved. The logic worked; everyone was satisfied. The gun must have been made by Lukens.

---

[8] The author pleads guilty to this as well. The original of this chapter, written before Carrick's article, is currently in the circular file.

[9] "A Great Curiosity," Discovering Lewis and Clark, http://lewis-clark.org/content/content-article.asp?ArticleID=1826.

Various researchers have suggested that Lukens made eight air guns during the period leading up to Lewis's time in Philadelphia. Four, perhaps five, of them are still extant. So, after Stewart found that Lewis's air gun still existed in 1846, and everyone interested settled on the gun being a Lukens, experts began to examine the possible guns. And there the journals enter the story again. On June 10, 1805 Lewis wrote, "The day being fair and fine we dryed all our baggage and merchandize. Shields renewed the main Spring of my air gun."[10] Experts examined the surviving Lukens air guns, looking for nonoriginal parts. And they found them.

The Virginia Military Institute (VMI) has a good collection of air guns, two of which are Lukens air guns from the late eighteenth or early nineteenth century. All of the known Lukens air guns are, as one would expect from a maker of fine clocks, elegant and refined, inside and out. They look like Pennsylvania rifles except that they have no pans and frizzens. The hammers are the beautiful serpentine design we associate with the Pennsylvania Rifles. All but one. That one, in the VMI collection, has a more robust, double-neck hammer of the type associated with military weapons. The mainspring too is crude, the kind of work a good blacksmith might do if he was working without a decent shop. Lewis had brought along a number of spare locks and parts from Harper's Ferry. Within a few months of Lewis's leaving there, the Harper's Ferry Arsenal was producing the Model 1803 Rifle with double-neck hammers. All the pieces fit. The VMI gun, it was assumed, must be the one Lewis took to the Pacific and back.

The puzzle was seemingly solved on the eve of the expedition's bicentennial. Then Michael Carrick published his paper on the Thomas Rodney description of Lewis's air rifle. The flaw in the train of logic was suddenly clear. Everyone had assumed that because Lukens ended up with the gun, he had made it. But if Lukens made the gun Thomas Rodney described, not only is it lost to us, it is radically different from any of the surviving Lukens air

---

[10]Moulton, *Journals of the Lewis and Clark Expedition*, 4:275.

guns. All of his that remain are single-shot muzzle loaders. Rodney describes a repeating weapon. There were a number of designs for repeating air guns at the beginning of the nineteenth century. But Rodney's account strongly suggests the type designed by G. C. Girandoni (a.k.a. Girardoni or Girardony) for the Austrian army.

Europe was not politically stable during the eighteenth and early nineteenth centuries. Austria fought wars against the Ottoman Empire, the Holy Roman Empire (and following its demise, Prussia), various powers in Italy and the Low Countries, and a whole series with France following the French Revolution and the rise of Napoleon. One result of all those wars was a large and well-financed military. Girandoni designed weapons for the Austrian military during the last quarter of the eighteenth century. His experiments with a repeating flintlock resulted in the loss of his left hand when a malfunction caused a test weapon to explode while he was firing it. He had better luck when he adapted the system to a repeating air rifle in the late 1770s. The result was the Model 1780. That weapon was improved, and the Model 1799 was the weapon that supposedly so upset Napoleon. It is unclear whether Girandoni was the lead manufacturer once he finished the design work. The fact that there were clearly many makers in Austria, Russia, Switzerland, England, and various German principalities using his design points to him as primarily an innovator that others then manufactured.[11]

A few of Girandoni's repeating air rifles have survived, and they are striking-looking weapons, with full-length forearms, very high, prominent hammers, and leather-covered metal stocks. On a Girandoni, as on many air guns of the time, the stock is the gun's air reservoir and detaches from the breech so it can be pumped up. It took five hundred to a thousand strokes of a hand pump to fill the air chamber to about 750 psi, but the gun can then be fired twenty to forty times. (The Austrian army supplied a larger pump mounted on a cart to facilitate refilling the air reservoirs.) Along the right side of the gun barrel, immediately

---

[11]Smith, *Gas, Air and Spring Guns of the World*, 28–30.

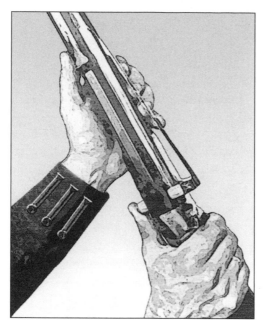

LOADING THE
GIRANDONI AIR RIFLE
This shows a soldier loading
the rifle by pushing the
breech block to the right
with his thumb. This must be
done while holding the rifle
vertically, as the balls feed
down the magazine by gravity.
Courtesy Michael F. Carrick.

in front of the hammer, is a tube about a foot long and about a half inch in diameter, capable of holding about twenty rifle balls. The front of the tube is gated, and a leaf spring, attached just behind the gate, runs slightly more than the length of the tube along its right side. There is a sliding breech block that sticks out on both sides of the weapon. The right side of the block closes the back of the tube magazine, its right edge in contact with the magazine's leaf spring. The left side projects from the weapon roughly an inch and a half to two inches.

When the rifleman pushes that block to the right, it moves against the spring and places a funnel-shaped hole in the block over the end of the magazine. The hole is large enough in the front for a ball to enter and too small in the back for the ball to fall through—but large enough for air to pass. By holding the rifle muzzle up the shooter allows gravity to drop a ball into the breechblock's hole. When the block is then released from the

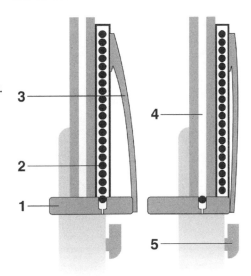

SCHEMATIC OF THE
GIRANDONI AIR RIFLE
(1) breech block; (2) magazine
(filled with balls); (3) leaf
spring; (4) barrel; (5) hammer.
By pushing the breech block
to the right while holding the
rifle in a barrel-up position,
the leaf spring is displaced to
the right and a ball falls into
the breechblock. Releasing
the block, the leaf spring
pushes the block back,
positioning the ball in line
with the barrel and the air
cylinder to the rear. *Courtesy
Michael F. Carrick.*

left, the leaf spring forces the block back to the left and the hole
containing the ball is moved back in line with the rifle barrel.
The shooter then cocks the hammer and air is released from the
reservoir into a chamber between the stock and the breech block
until the pressure in the two chambers is equalized. Then the
reservoir valve closes. (The failure of this valve from something
as insignificant as a bit of dirt could easily explain the problem
of the weapon when Lewis was demonstrating it to Thomas
Rodney.) Pulling the trigger then opens the valve at the front
of the forward air chamber, and the air pressure sends the ball
down the barrel at a speed of several hundred feet per second.

Lewis's first journal entry does state that he had purchased the
air gun, but neither that or any evidence has surfaced to explain
exactly where or when he acquired it. There is no other good
evidence for Girandoni-style air rifles having made it to the
United States by the beginning of the nineteenth century. Since
so many different manufacturers in so many different countries
were producing the weapons, it is easy to imagine them being

traded widely and without great comment during the more than twenty years from the weapon's introduction in 1780 until Lewis headed west. Interestingly enough, Lewis's penultimate journal entry also mentions the air rifle and another shooting accident as well. On that day, after being shot by Cruzatte, Lewis assumed that he and Cruzatte had been attacked by a party of Indians, and he called out to Cruzatte, who failed to respond. He made his way back to the river and called to his men to aid him in his attempt to save Cruzatte from the supposed Indian attack. The ball that wounded Lewis had passed through both cheeks of his buttocks, and Lewis found:

> my wounds became so painfull and my thye so stiff that I could scarcely get on; in short I was compelled to halt and ordered the men to proceed and if they found themselves overpowered by numbers to retreat in order keeping up a fire. I now got back to the perogue as well as I could and prepared myself with a pistol my rifle and air-gun being determined as retreat was impracticable to sell my life as deerly as possible.
>
> *Lewis, August 11, 1806*[12]

If Lewis's air gun was capable of firing twenty shots in a minute, his defense would likely have been as effective as it was heroic. As events unfolded, the men returned with Cruzatte, who at least pretended bafflement, claiming he had never fired his rifle. Lewis had the ball that wounded him, one of the same caliber as the short rifle Cruzatte carried. Lewis was sure he had been shot accidentally by his one-eyed, nearsighted companion, but, somewhat uncharacteristically, he dropped the matter.

In between those incidents of April 1803 and August 1806, the air rifle is mentioned twenty times. In sixteen of those instances the air rifle was shot as a demonstration to impress various tribes. Since not every journalist mentions these performances on the same days, it seems reasonable to assume the weapon might have been fired more often than that. It may be that it became such a routine piece of equipment to the Corps that the writers didn't

---

[12]Moulton, *Journals of the Lewis and Clark Expedition*, 8:155.

deem it necessary to note its every use. For instance, neither Sergeant Gass nor Private Whitehouse ever mentions it. The various tribes all seem to have had the same reaction to the air rifle. Most of the journals describe the tribes as astonished or surprised. On January 24, 1806, Lewis wrote his longest report on the Indians' reaction to the air gun. "My Air-gun also astonishes them very much, they cannot comprehend it's shooting so often and without powder; and think that it is *great medicine* which comprehends every thing that is to them incomprehensible."[13] The line "shooting so often" seems to support the idea that Lewis had a repeating air rifle such as a Girandoni type.

The final mention of the air rifle in the journals is undated. After returning to St. Louis, some of Clark's notes refer to the air rifle being boxed for shipment back East.[14] Then, as the trackers say, the trail goes cold. But rather than turn away, it is useful to look at one last piece of evidence. Isaiah Lukens's estate papers say that the air gun was not only carried by Lewis but made for him as well. By whom? Based on whose design? Did Lewis acquire the designs for a Girandoni and take them to Pennsylvania and have one made for the trip? Did Lukens, after all, make Lewis's air gun, but not from his standard model? Or did the writer of the estate sale brochure make a small literary error and add "made for" to "used"? Had Lukens only acquired it after Lewis's death? Did he want it because of where it had been or because he wanted to study the unusual design? Or . . . ?

The Corps of Discovery's expedition was one of the best documented of the period, but there are many questions about it that are probably unanswerable two hundred years later. What exactly Lewis's air gun was may well be one of those questions. But historians should be wary of the word "never."

---

[13]Ibid., 6:233.
[14]Ibid., 8:419.

CHAPTER 7

Edged Weapons

I f the Corps of Discovery's firearms were a means of feeding
and defending itself, the members' edged weapons were their
last line of defense, their everyday tools, and valuable trade
items. The Corps was as well supplied with edged weapons as it
was with firearms. Everyone in the permanent party was issued
a knife and a tomahawk. As officers, Lewis and Clark each had a
sword. Lewis, an infantry officer, also had an espontoon, and it is
possible that Clark, though an artillery officer, may have had one
too, since his former commission was in the infantry. The men
who had come from line companies and brought their Model
1795 muskets had bayonets as well. What these various weapons
were and how they were used are questions whose answers are
less obvious today than they were two hundred years ago, enough
so that it is worth looking at each in turn.

Lewis and Clark were both officers in the U.S. Army. That
gave them some privileges as well as many responsibilities. A
commission in the army at the beginning of the nineteenth century bestowed two ranks on a man, that of an officer and that of
a gentleman. Though the Revolution, fought a quarter century
earlier, had made it clear that the country would have no inher-
ited aristocracy, a gentleman was still considered a step above
the masses. The big difference here was that a person could move
from one class to another. One of the privileges of an officer was
to wear that ancient accouterment of a gentleman's position, the
sword. For centuries, the sword had been the mark of station as
well as rank. According to Clegg Furr, Lewis and Clark should

have had recognizably different swords. Since officers purchased their own swords, there was some individual variation. But there were regulations. Lewis, an infantry captain, should have had, following the 1801 regulations, a "white mounted sword with [a] cut and thrust blade[s] . . . 28 inches long." Clark, as a lieutenant of artillery, would have had, according to those same regulations, a yellow-mounted sword with a cut-and-thrust blade. But Clark was already at Camp Dubois when his commission came, so he likely had the sword from his previous service. Since he had held a staff position in an infantry unit originally, he could have had either a three-foot-long saber with iron or steel mountings as per the 1787 regulations for infantry officers, or following the requirements for a staff officer, whatever he chose. Since there was considerable leeway given officers in their choice of swords, it seems unlikely that we can say anything more definite than that their swords were twenty-eight to thirty-nine inches long with either curved or straight blades and may have been either iron, steel, or white (bone or ivory) mounted.[1]

The sword was never as important a weapon in the United States as it was in Europe. On the frontier in particular, the sword, while still a mark of a gentleman, was not very practical as a tool and an absolute nuisance while walking off trail in the forest. Through the eighteenth century, the tomahawk gradually replaced the sword along the American frontier. But in the nineteenth century's first decade, the sword was still both a symbol of rank and, in trained hands, a superb weapon for close combat. For instance, during the standoff with the Teton Sioux in October 1804, Clark drew his sword to demonstrate his willingness to take the issue to final conclusions if needed. Yet less than two years later, on April 28, 1806, Clark traded off his sword for a horse. By then Clark certainly needed no symbol of his rank, if ever he did; he seems to have been the type of officer with whom the enlisted men and other officers dream of serving. In all probability he recognized that he was unlikely to need his sword again and he knew how badly the Corps needed horses.

---

[1]Furr, *American Swords and Makers' Marks*, 6–10.

Given that he had unsuccessfully tried twice to trade his sword for a horse the week before (April 20 and 25), it seems that he was not the only one who felt that horses were more valuable.

The standoff with the Tetons transpired, according to Clark's journal, in this fashion:

> I went with those Cheifs [NB: in one of the Pirogues with 5 men 3 & 2 Ints][2] (which left the boat with great reluctance) to Shore with a view of reconseleing those men to us, as Soon as I landed the Perogue three of their young men Seased the Cable of the Perogue   [NB: in which we had presents &c.], the Chiefs Soldr. [NB: each Chief has a Soldier] Huged the mast, and the 2d Chief was verry insolent both in words and justures [NB: pretended drunkness & staggered up against us] declareing I Should not go on, Stateing he had not recved presents Suffient from us, his justures were of Such a personal nature I felt my Self Compeled to Draw my Sword, [NB: and made a Signal to the boat to prepar for action] at this motion Capt. Lewis ordered all under arms in the boat, those with me   also Showed a Disposition to Defend themselves and me, the grand Chief then took hold of the roop & ordered the young warrers away, I felt my Self warm & Spoke in verry positive terms.
>
> *Clark, September 25, 1804*[3]

The return of a pirogue with twelve heavily armed men and the preparations of the other thirty plus men, including the loading of the swivel gun and the blunderbusses, probably were more intimidating than Clark's sword. But the act of drawing it, in the face of overwhelming numbers, certainly told the Tetons in general, and the chief in reach of it in particular, that the Corps of Discovery was not a group that would allow itself to be trifled with. As a British general once noted, cold steel and hot blood were two principal ingredients of empire. Clark would certainly have admitted to having his blood up at the time. The sword was just the expression of his will.

Three days later, according to Whitehouse's journal, Lewis drew his sword in a less remembered encounter with the Tetons.

---

[2]The comments designated [NB:] are, to quote Moulton, "Nicholas Biddle's emendations or interlineations." *Journals of the Lewis & Clark Expedition*.

[3]Moulton, *Journals of the Lewis and Clark Expedition*, 3:113.

During that confrontation, Lewis only mentions taking the port fire from the gunner, threatening the men who held the boat's cable with a blast from the swivel. Whitehouse, who hadn't mentioned Clark's sword on September 25 (perhaps he was not in a position to see that part of the action), wrote:

> when we were about to Shove off a nomber of warries on Shore caught hold of our cable and another whiped of[f] the children   the women off also only   about 60 warries on the edge of the bank and we just under the bank.   Some of them had fire arms and the rest had Good bows and arrows ready for war.   the consequences had like to have ben bad as Capt. Lewis was near cutting the cable with his Sword and giving orders for the party to fire on them.   then the chiefs went out and Spoke to them.   they   Said if we would Give them a carrit of tobacco they would loose the rope.   we gave them tobacco.   the chief after Some hesitation loosed the rope himself.   we then Set of[f].
>
> *Whitehouse, September 28, 1804*[4]

There are no other records of a sword being drawn in anger. It fits nicely with the evolving myth of the West that in the one fight the Corps had with Indians, the one with the Blackfeet in 1806, Lewis had a pistol as a sidearm, not a sword. Yet swords should not be thought of as unimportant in the West. On at least five occasions, on both the Missouri and the Columbia, members of the Corps reported encountering Indians armed with swords. Around the mouth of the Columbia trade with coasting vessels provided many opportunities for acquiring swords and cutlasses, which were often listed in trade manifests.[5] But some of the swords the Corps found along the Columbia were not from obvious trade sources. The most interesting of these weapons, "iron scimitars" as the journalists called them, were reported on March 29, 1806. The Corps had left Fort Clatsop, the tiny fort they had built in the fall of 1805 near the mouth of the Columbia River, on March 23. Six days later they arrived at a "Cath-lab-poh-tle" village, where they found the people had

---

[4]Ibid., 11:89–90.
[5]Gibson, *Otter Skins, Boston Ships & China Goods*.

a number of large symeters of Iron from 3 to 4 feet long which hang by the heads of their beads; the blades of this weapon is thickest in the center tho' thin even there.   all it's edges are sharp and it's greatest width which is about 9 inches from the point is about 4 inches.   the form is thus.   this is a formidable weapon.

Lewis, March 29, 1806[6]

The statement "the form is thus" is followed by Lewis's attempt to illustrate the weapon. Clark's copy of this part of Lewis's journal is somewhat different.

John Ordway's journal ends with a couple of pages of undated notes that includes a list of things that he felt would be useful in the Pacific trade. Two of the things mentioned are "Swords and big knives."[7] All in all it seems that while swords were good trade items, they were not thought to be as useful as many other tools or weapons.

If the members of the Corps felt swords to be unimportant, they all apparently put great store in their tomahawks. The name "tomahawk" is derived from an Algonquian word for a type of war club.[8] English speakers quickly adopted the word and by the late seventeenth century had changed its meanings so that it meant any metal-headed, lightweight ax. As tribes traded for European and later American-produced tomahawks, the head designs changed over time and depending on the country of origin. Styles varied from a simple hatchet type to spike and hammer headed to espontoon. One of the most popular designs at the beginning of the nineteenth century was the pipe toma-hawk, a design that combined a smoking pipe bowl on one side of the head with a hatchet blade on the other. An interesting aspect of this design is that it incorporates both the ax blade of war and action and the pipe bowl of peaceful conversation and contemplation—a tool of many uses and many moods.

[6]Moulton, *Journals of the Lewis and Clark Expedition*, 7:28.
[7]Ibid., 9:368–69.
[8]Peterson, *American Indian Tomahawk*, 4.

By the eighteenth century, American colonial militias had largely replaced their swords with tomahawks. Since the militia members had to supply their weapons, this was logical both in terms of cost and in familiarity. To use any weapon effectively requires practice. It was much easier to practice with a weapon one handled in everyday routines. As Harold Peterson points out, "During the Revolutionary War regular infantry generally abandoned the hatchet, but light infantry and riflemen who did not have bayonets continued to carry tomahawks throughout the conflict."[9]

Tomahawks were a great all-purpose tool/weapon in the eastern woodlands. They were less practical on the Great Plains, where there were few trees except along the streams. The members of the Corps of Discovery were from the East and brought their accustomed tools and weapons. Peterson's research revealed that in 1793 the various U.S. arsenals listed over 2,300 tomahawks in their inventory.[10] Yet, a decade later, Lewis had tomahawks made for the Corps of Discovery to use and to trade. Records don't reveal whether any of the 2,300 were at Harper's Ferry in 1803. If they were, Lewis may still have had tomahawks of a different design, such as pipe tomahawks, made for the expedition.

According to Donald Jackson, Lewis figured he would need two dozen pipe tomahawks for the expedition members and another three dozen for "Indian Presents." The document shows that the thirty-six were needed as Indian presents, and Lewis noted that they were to be prepared at the Harper's Ferry Arsenal.[11] In the list of "Supplies from Private Vendors," Jackson shows that Lewis noted that "Nich. Lloyd" was paid $19.62 for tomahawks. Jackson notes that Lloyd was the only Philadelphia merchant for whom the individual voucher has never been identified. There was, again according to Jackson's research, a blacksmith named Nicodemus Lloyd who conducted his business at

---

[9]Ibid., 41.
[10]Ibid.
[11]Jackson, *Letters of the Lewis and Clark Expedition*, items 53–57.

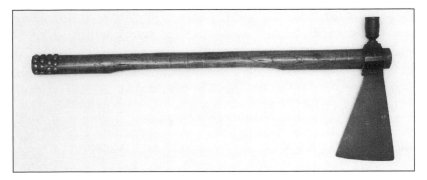

PIPE TOMAHAWK

While this tomahawk is from a bit later time, the design was well established by the beginning of the nineteenth century. It was a useful tool for work, war, ceremony, and contemplation. Some of the expedition members carried their own, and Lewis had some made for use and for trade. *Courtesy Buffalo Bill Historical Center, Cody, Wyoming, U.S.A.; Chandler-Pohrt Collection, NA.504.258.*

7th and Sassafras Streets in Philadelphia during 1803. He would have been the most likely one to have made the tomahawks.[12] The "Summary of Purchases" indicates twelve pipe tomahawks were purchased for $18.00. Five pages later Lewis indicates that he received eighteen tomahawks from public stores. This same is acknowledged as having been delivered to Lewis "from the Arsenal."[13] One cannot tell from this whether or not these are pipe tomahawks. These records are so vague that it is difficult to tell exactly how many tomahawks Lewis finally packed into the keelboat when he headed West. For our purposes it seems safe to say, "Enough."

At the time he was gathering equipment in the East, Lewis was still thinking of an expedition of about fifteen men. The eighteen tomahawks he drew from army stores would then have constituted enough for the Corps members plus two or three

[12]Ibid., item 57:93.
[13]Ibid., item 57:98.

extra for trade. The fact that the expedition was over twice that size could explain why members were sent back to find lost tomahawks on most occasions. We do not know what Lewis's tomahawk looked like. We do know that it was lost by Sergeant Gass. Lewis recorded the incident on August 2, 1805, writing, "I regret the loss of this useful implement, however accedents will happen in the best families, and I consoled myself with the recollection that it was not the only one we had with us."[14] Lewis's taking the loss of his personal tomahawk so easily says much about his regard for Sergeant Gass. It also suggests that the Corps still had spares at that point. It further suggests that some of the men brought their own tomahawks with them on the expedition.

Almost certainly the nine young men from Kentucky brought their own arms and accouterments with them; young men from Kentucky at the beginning of the nineteenth century would have thought of their weapons as tools without which they were not prone to leave home. The arms belonging to frontiersmen from the woodlands would have included tomahawks. We do know from the journals that Sergeant Floyd, one of the nine young men, had a personal tomahawk and shot pouch. While it is safe to assume that these men had tomahawks, there is no evidence of styles. We do know that the army was not issuing tomahawks to troops. At the time, the Model 1795 musket was the standard issue firearm, and it came with a bayonet, the Army's preferred weapon for close combat. Since some of the troops who joined the Corps of Discovery had some frontier experience in or out of the army, it is possible they had included tomahawks in their personal gear. Sergeant Gass, for instance, had come to the regular army from a volunteer ranger unit, many of which were armed with tomahawks. It is possible he brought more than knowledge of the tool/weapon with him. But since no evidence survives to support such a suggestion about Gass or any other member transferred to the Corps from another unit, it may be safer for

---

[14]Moulton, *Journals of the Lewis and Clark Expedition*, 5:32.

a historian to assume they did not arrive at Camp Dubois so accoutered. The same is true for the engagés. There is no indication of how they were equipped before joining the expedition.

Tomahawks were lost on eleven recorded occasions. At first glance, this implies carelessness on the part of the Corps, but for a group of over thirty men who spent over thirty months in a wide variety of circumstances, the loss is understandable. On five of those occasions the tomahawks were recovered, and on two more the journals are unclear. There were five attempts to steal tomahawks from the Corps. Twice these were successful, although when Clark's was stolen on November 4, 1805, John Colter recovered it on the following April 9. The fact that Colter recognized the pipe tomahawk five months later would seem to indicate that it was at least somewhat personalized.

On three occasions tomahawks were traded, twice for horses and once for a different pipe. That occasion was only two days after Colter recovered Clark's pipe. The Corps, while portaging the Cascades of the Columbia, was having trouble with Watlala Indians ("Wah-clel-lahs," in Lewis's spelling). Various members of the tribe had attempted to steal some of the Corps's things, including Lewis's dog. One of the chiefs worked hard at making peace and revealed to the captains the extent of coastal trade between Indians and whites.

> The Chief appeared mortified at the conduct of his people, and seemed friendly disposed towards us.   as he appeared to be a man of consideration as we had reason to believe much rispected by the neighbouring tribes we thought it well to bestoe a medal of small size on him.   he appeared much gratifyed with this mark of distinction, and some little attention which we showed him.   he had in his possession a very good pipe tomahawk which he informed us he had received as a present from a trader who visited him last winter over land pointing to the N. W. whome he called Swippeton; he was pleased with the tomahawk of Capt. C. in consequence of it's having a brass   bowl and Capt. C. gratified him by an exchange.
>
> *Lewis, April 11, 1806*[15]

---

[15]Ibid., 7:106.

Not only does this passage illustrate the importance of trade as part of diplomacy but it hints at how extensive coastal trade already was. It is impossible to tell from the chief's description if he had journeyed to the coast to trade, if he had met a trader partway to the coast, or if some unrecorded trader, Swippeton by name, had already penetrated as far up the Columbia as the Cascades.

With all the obvious interest in tomahawks evidenced by the Corps—in the numbers they thought they would need, in the officers' willingness to send men back to look for lost ones, and in their efforts to recover stolen ones—there is remarkably little reference to their actual use. There are no clear references in the entire year of 1804, one in 1805 (when the men killed several otters with their tomahawks), and three times in 1806 (to blaze trail, to threaten to destroy a canoe rather than give it up without trade, and once when Lewis offered to split open a Nez Perce man's head for making fun of Lewis eating a dog). It also seems likely that the trailblazing on the Lolo Trail over the Bitterroots in 1805 was done with tomahawks, though they are not specifically mentioned.

It is also of interest that except for the attempted theft of one or more tomahawks by some Sioux, who were trying to take everything, not just tomahawks, all the thefts and attempted thefts were by tribes who had access to forests. The tomahawk makes more sense if thought of as both tool and weapon and is more likely to be thought of as such by forest people.

The Mandans, certainly not a forest people, loved tomahawks, but only the ones they had John Shields build for them during the winter of 1804–1805. Some of these were simple ax blades designed for work, but most were of elaborate ceremonial design of the half pike or espontoon form. While these could be most formidable weapons, the evidence from a variety of sources over the next two or three decades is that they were mainly used for symbolism and ceremony. They certainly were not useful as tools, as hatchets. During the winter, John Shields was able to secure for the expedition considerable amounts of corn by making and trading these tomahawk heads to just about anyone with the asking price. The Mandans would have made Shields a wealthy man had he stayed with them and opened a blacksmith shop there, and his tomahawk design was so popular that he made enough for the Corps to take West for trade. On August 25, 1805, Lewis offered some of these "battle axes," as he called them, to the Shoshones for horses. The Shoshones liked them, but Lewis had to add a knife, a handkerchief, and some paint to come up with the price of a horse.

There are some journal entries concerning tomahawks that are interesting comments on human nature. On June 1, 1806, when Clark was copying Lewis's journal, almost word for word, both mention looking for two tomahawks lost or stolen in the area the year before. Lewis had written, "the one is a tomahawk which Capt. C. Left at our Camp on Musquetor Creek."[16] Clark copies, "one is a pipe tomahawk which Capt. L left at our Camp on Musquetor Creek."[17] The year before, on October 7, Clark, after commenting on the ill health of the group from eating too much camas root, wrote, "I also missed my Pipe tomahawk which could not be found."[18] He is noncommittal about how it came to be missing.

Another entry about tomahawks, which follows the captains' writings of June 1, 1806, suggests the value we can place on things far beyond their intrinsic worth. The lost tomahawks had been located, and Drouillard was sent to recover them.

> Drewyer arrived this evening with Neeshneparkeeook and Hohashill-pilp   who had accompanied him to the lodge of the person who had our tomahawks   he obtained both the tomahawks principally by the influence of the former of those Chiefs.   the one which had been Stolen we prized most as it was the private property of the late Serjt. Floyd and I was desireous of returning it to his friends. The man who had this tomahawk had purchased it from the man who had

[16]Ibid., 7:322.
[17]Ibid., 7:324–25.
[18]Ibid., 5:249.

Stolen it, and was himself at the moment of their arrival just expiring.   his relations were unwilling to give up the tomahawk as they intended to bury it with the deceased owner, but were at length to do so for the Consideration of a handkerchief, two Strands of beeds, which drewyer gave them and two horses given by the Chiefs to be   Killed agreeable to their custom at the grave of the deceased.

Clark, June 2, 1806[19]

So it appears that George Drouillard, a name we have seen that Clark usually rendered as "Drewyer," gifted hand talker and good diplomat, was able, with the assistance of two Nez Perces of the same nature, to reconcile the Corps's desire to return their dead sergeant's personal pipe tomahawk to his friends with the Nez Perce desire to bury a man with a prized possession.

If tomahawks were not fully appreciated by all the tribes the Corps of Discovery met during its journey, steel knives were. Lewis knew that as he planned the trip with Jefferson, and not only did his estimate of equipment needed list two dozen large knives for the arms and accouterments, it listed 36 large knives and 288 "Knives Small as are generally used for the Indian trade, with fix'd blades & handles inlaid with brass" as "Indian Presents." When he was shopping in Philadelphia, Lewis received from John and Charles J. Wister four dozen butcher knives, which he showed as Indian presents. These cost eleven cents each. Either from the Wisters or from another merchant Lewis acquired eleven dozen slightly larger knives costing nineteen cents each.[20]

Lewis also drew fifteen "Scalping Knives & Belts" from public stores.[21] That only fifteen such knives were made for Lewis at Harper's Ferry indicates that, at that time, May of 1803, he was still planning a small expedition. The knives were, according to Lewis, excellent knives, and two letters express his thinking. Lewis had forgotten his dirk at the White House. Jefferson

---

[19]Ibid., 7:328–29.
[20]Jackson, *Letters of the Lewis and Clark Expedition*, item 57:93, 94.
[21]Ibid., 57:98.

wrote to him on July 11, 1803, offering to send the knife by post. On July 22, Lewis replied, "Dirk could not well come by post, nor is it of any moment to me, the knives that were made at HF will answer my purpose equally as well and perhaps better, it can therefore be taken care of until my return."[22] In the chapter on personal weapons there are hints that Lewis might have purchased a dirk, perhaps in St. Louis, that he used for trade along the way. Was this the dirk that stayed behind, or one of the knives in the pistol case in Lewis's effects after his death?[23]

Those fifteen scalping knives were for the expedition members' use, though not for the use the name implies. Lewis either used one of these or purchased a dirk, and Clark wrote of his own dirk. It seems safe to assume that Drouillard and Charbonneau as well as the nine young men from Kentucky all had knives. The soldiers likely would have had some type of knife, either issued or acquired personally. On May 18, 1804, Clark wrote that he gave knives to three of the "French hands." That only three of the engagés needed knives indicates that most had blades adequate for the expedition. York, who had likely hunted all his life with Clark, would have had a knife as well as a rifle. Sacagawea would have had a knife, since it was a tool of everyday life for an Indian woman—and since her husband was, by the lights of the time and place, a wealthy man, she may well have had quite a good knife.

Only the Corps's primary knives were generally mentioned in the journals, but the expedition had a variety of other types of knives. For instance, on June 26, 1805, while men and gear were scattered along the seventeen-mile portage around the Great Falls of the Missouri, Lewis does comment that he had to bleed Joseph Whitehouse and nothing with which to do it but his pen knife, which "answered pretty well." In other words, Lewis didn't have his set of bleeding lancets—part of the medical kit assembled in Philadelphia with the help of Benjamin Rush—with him at the time.

---

[22]Ibid., item 75:111.
[23]Ibid., item 303:472.

The journals only mentioned three knives being lost, and two of those were recovered. In another case, some knives never mentioned as lost were returned by Indians. These, apparently, were some or all of the eleven table knives Lewis had acquired in Philadelphia.[24] Knives were so important that men were sent back to retrieve those left behind. The rule for doing so seems strict enough that Moses Reed used going back for his knife as the cover for his desertion on August 4, 1804. As Clark reminds us in his journal entry for August 7, the Corps of Discovery was a unit of the U.S. Army, and desertion was a serious offense. He had sent four men "back after the Deserter reid with order if he did not give up Peaceibly to put him to Death."[25] He did not need to add that they were to bring back his rifle and accouterments.

In addition to the knives being lost, there were six journal reports of knives being stolen, three of which were recovered, as well as reports of other attempted thefts that were foiled. It seems likely that the men, for the most part, had their knives with them at most times, so it would have been rare for a knife to have been someplace where it could have been stolen. There are also several mentions in the journals of knives being lent to Indians, all of which were returned promptly.

A half-dozen journal references to Indians in various parts of the West suggest that knives were an important trade item. Steel blades were obviously preferred to stone ones, not because of sharpness but because of durability; a good stone knife became dull fairly quickly, while a steel blade would last for many years. The expedition had at least 180 trade knives, of which the journals account for only about a third being traded off or given away. Yet on November 21, 1805, Clark wrote, "we divided Some ribin between the men of our party to bestow on their favorite Lasses, this plan to Save the Knives & more valuable articles."[26] This makes it appear that considerably more knives had been

[24]Ibid., item 55:83.
[25]Moulton, *Journals of the Lewis and Clark Expedition*, 2:455–56.
[26]Ibid., 6:74.

traded than had been recorded in the journals. The number of unrecorded trades didn't diminish the stock so much that there were none left for trade on the way back East, when they helped to secure some horse trades. The last record of a knife being traded or given as a gift was on June 13, 1806.

The styles of knives the Corps carried for trade were not the only ones available. Lewis indicates that tribes along the Columbia and Snake had come to like what "the Northwest traders call and eye-dag," described by Moulton as "a type of dagger or stabbing knife . . . a specimen is extant from the Northwest coast with a hole or eye in the handle for inserting a loop which would hold the knife around the wrist.[27] The preferred knife of the coastal tribes the Corps met was described by Clark:

> The form of a knife which Seems to be perfured by those people is a double Edged and double pointed dagger the handle being near the middle, the blades of unequal length, the longest from 9 to 10 incs. and the Shorter one from 3 to 5 inches.   those knives they Carry with them habitually and most usially in the hand.   Sometimes exposed, when in Company with Strangers under their Robes   with this knife they Cut & Clense their fish make their arrows &c.   this is the form of the knife [Clark's illustration inserted here, with "A" above a loop on the handle of the knife]   A is a Small loop of Strong twine thong through which they Sometimes they incert the thumb in order to prevent it being wrested from their hand.
>
> *Clark, January 29, 1806*[28]

There is no indication of where this design came from and with whom the tribes were trading to secure them.

There are few references to knives being used. Almost all of the uses were so routine as to not even be thought of, let alone written about. On two occasions we read of knives being used, or threatened to be used, as weapons. On April 11, 1806, up the Columbia from Beacon Rock, John Shields was behind the group, having stopped to buy a dog. Two Indians attempted to take the dog from him.

---

[27]Ibid., 8:135, 137n.
[28]Ibid., 6:246–48.

he had nothing to defend himself with except a large knife which he drew with an intention of puting one or both of them to death before they could get themselves in readiness to use their arrows, but discovering his design they declined the combat and instantly fled through the woods.

Lewis, April 11, 1806[29]

Just over three months later a knife was actually used as a weapon for the only time on the expedition. In the fight with the Blackfeet during Lewis's Marias River survey, Reuben Field wrestled with one of the young Indians for his rifle and stabbed the man in the heart. The simple, straightforward solution was the one taken, kill the man rather than humiliate him.

Twice the journals record men using knives to save themselves from falls. On May 23, 1804, Lewis slipped on a rain-soaked hillside and almost plunged off a cliff into the Missouri, but he used his knife to arrest his slide before he went over the edge. There isn't a clear telling of what happened because Lewis either wasn't writing in his journal at that time or the pages are missing. Clark, however, offers one of his inimitable descriptions: "Capt Lewis' ascended the hill which has peninsulis projecting in raged points to the river, and was near falling from a Peninsulia   *hard water all Day*   Saved himself by the assistance of his Knife."[30] Just over a year later, Lewis was leading a group along a bluff above the Missouri when he and another man, Richard Windsor, slipped. Lewis's journal leaves us with a much better account than Clark's of the year before.

> In passing along the face of one of these bluffs today I sliped at a narrow pass of about 30 yards in length and but for a quick and fortunate recovery by means of my espontoon I should been percipitated into the river down a craggy pricipice of about ninety feet. I had scarcely reached a place on which I could stand with tolerable safety even with the assistance of my espontoon before I heard a voice behind me cry out god god Capt. what shall I do   on turning about I found it was Windsor who had sliped and fallen abut the center of this narrow pass

---

[29]Ibid., 7:105.
[30]Ibid., 2:248.

and was lying prostrate on his belley, with his [one] wright hand arm
and leg over the precipice while he was holding on with the left arm
and foot as well as he could which appeared to be with much difficulty.
I discovered his danger and the trepedation which he was in gave me
still further concern for I expected every instant to see him loose his
strength and slip off; altho' much allarmed at his situation I disguised
my feelings and spoke very calmly to him and assured him that he was
in no kind of danger, to take the knife out of his belt behind him with
his wright hand and dig a hole with it in the face of the bank to receive
his wright foot which he did and then raised himself to his knees; I
then directed him to take off his mockersons and to come forward on
his hands and knees holding the knife in one hand and the gun in the
other   this he happily effected and escaped.   those who were
some little distance bhind returned by my orders and waded the river
at the foot of the bluff where the water was breast deep.

Lewis, June 7, 1805[31]

On two occasions men cut themselves badly enough with their
knives to merit mention in the journals. Oddly enough, these
two incidents happened within five weeks of each other in the
summer of 1806. On one occasion Lewis wrote:

we had not proceeded far this morning before Potts (John
Potts)   cut his leg very badly with one of the large knives; he cut
one of the large veigns on the inner side of the leg; I found much difficulty in stoping the blood which I could not effect untill I applyed
a tight bandage with a little cushon of wood and tow on the veign
below the wound.

Lewis, June 18, 1806[32]

Ordway's journal adds that Lewis took stitches. Just over a
month later, on July 23, while the men prepared to leave the
Great Falls to meet Lewis at the Marias, Ordway wrote, "Wiser
(Peter Weiser) cut his leg with a knife So that he is unable to
walk & is a bod wound."[33] The wounds proved not to be serious
as they first appeared, and the men recovered quickly and with
no complications.

---

[31]Ibid., 4:262–63.
[32]Ibid., 8:35.
[33]Ibid., 9:340.

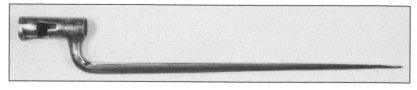

BAYONET

The soldiers who brought muskets with them from their previous commands would have had bayonets such as this 1795 model. It would have slid over the end of the musket barrel with the blade above the barrel, then been rotated to the right and back so that the front sight would have fit into the slot visible in the picture. The blade would have then been on the right side, allowing the soldier still to reach the ramrod under the barrel. *Courtesy Michael F. Carrick.*

Twice there are references to knives that can only be described as unusual. Ordway uses the knife as a symbol for peace, referring to burying the knife rather than the hatchet, as the phrase usually goes. And on October 12, 1804, when an Arikara man was offered a drink, he responded that whiskey is so bad for people that they would have to give him a knife first as payment for his acting crazy once the alcohol was in his system. These two instances give us an idea of the ubiquitous nature of the knife. It was such an essential tool that it would have been used numerous times each day, yet knives are only mentioned in the unusual circumstances of accidents or when used as a weapon.

The bayonet, on the other hand, is mentioned only four times. The journals record drilling with bayoneted muskets and a bayonet's being found, though there's no mention of its having been lost in the first place, and there are two references to bayonets being attached to poles and used as fishing gigs, infrequency that probably has more to do with the bayonet's being so unnecessary as a weapon that no one ever thinks about it. The members of the Corps drawn from line companies came to the expedition with full arms and accouterments of an infantry or artillery soldier of the day, and in both cases that would have included a Model 1795 and its bayonet.

The bayonet had a triangular blade designed for stabbing, not for slashing, with no cutting edge and no handle; it could not, as could those of a century later, be substituted for a knife. The blade attached to the musket's barrel via a sleeve. The sleeve was slotted, and the barrel had a lug along the bottom so the bayonet could be slid on and rotated ninety degrees to lock in place. This rotation not only locked the bayonet to the barrel but moved the bayonet out of line, with the ram pipe carried below the barrel. Bayonets of the period were fifteen to twenty-four inches long. Mounted on a five-foot-long musket, a bayonet made it a spear six feet long, and presented en masse by a line of battle-grimed soldiers marching to the attack, was a formidable weapon.

Such intimidation was a bayonet's real function, demonstrated when Lewis and Clark drilled their men for the tribes during the summer of 1804—the last mention of the bayonet in the journals. Even fifteen men in matching uniforms, all armed with bayoneted muskets and so well supplied with ammunition that they could fire a volley for show and then level those long weapons at the crowd, was a power to be reckoned with. Cold steel and hot blood were indeed the stuff of empire.

Of all the weapons carried by the Corps of Discovery, probably the least understood two hundred years later is the espontoon. Even its spelling and pronunciation cause problems. There are references in the period to "espontoon," "espantoon" (Lewis uses both), "spontoon," "espotoon," and "espatoon." Clark, with his obvious spelling problems, limits himself to "spear." The other term for the weapon is "half pike." It was issued to lieutenants and some captains of the day as walking stick, defensive weapon, and easily seen mark of rank, and it consisted of a hardwood shaft about six feet long, metal bound on the foot to prevent wearing away and/or splitting and the head mounting a spear. The spear head was distinctive and appealing. The style of tomahawk that most of the Mandans wanted John Shields to make for them during the winter of 1805–1806 was often called an "espontoon tomahawk," the head being shaped more like the spear head of a espontoon than an axe, though still set at a right angle to the handle.

Lewis used his espontoon mainly as a walking stick, but he refers to it saving him during the incident on June 7, 1805, when he slipped on the bluff along the Missouri. The espontoon served other less serious purposes as well. On May 14, 1805, Lewis was examining a pair of porcupines and noted that they were "exceedingly clumsy and not very watchfull I approached so near one of them before it percieved me that I touched it with my espontoon."[34] He wrote on May 12, 1805, "in these excurtions I most generally went alone armed with my rifle and espontoon; thus equiped I feel myself more than an equal match for a brown bear provided I get him in the open woods."[35] A month later, along the Missouri near the Great Falls, when he did have his close encounter with a grizzly, once he was in water deep enough for him to stand but so deep that the bear was required to swim, he felt able to defend himself with his espontoon. Yet, as pleased as he was with his espontoon, Lewis reloaded his rifle as soon as he returned to shore, even though he could see the bear running three miles away.

A bit less than a month before the above (May 26, 1805) incident, Lewis had stepped past a rattlesnake and narrowly missed being bitten. Lewis then "struck about at random . . . with my espontoon being directed in some measure by his nois untill I killed him."[36] Three days later Lewis wrote that Clark killed a wolf with "his espontoon."[37] On the same day Clark wrote that "I

[34]Ibid., 4:104.
[35]Ibid., 4:145.
[36]Ibid., 4:201–202.
[37]Ibid., 4:217.

ESPONTOON

This combination spear and walking stick was a badge of rank, carried by officers. It was roughly six and a half feet long. *Courtesy Michael F. Carrick.*

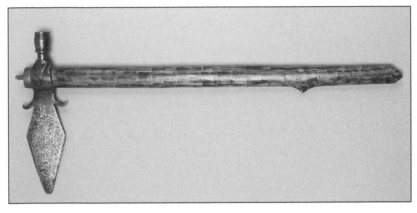

ESPONTOON-HEADED TOMAHAWK

John Shields made many tomahawks similar to this one, though without the attached pipe, for trade with the Mandans during the winter of 1804–1805. While not as useful as the hatchet head design, the Mandans seemingly considered them a status symbol. *Courtesy Buffalo Bill Historical Center, Cody, Wyoming, U.S.A.; Chandler-Pohrt Collection, NA.504.257.*

walked on \<shore\> the bank in the evening and saw the remains of a number of buffalow, which had been drove down a Clift of rocks . . . Great numbers of wolves were about this place & verry jentle   I killed one of them with my Spear."[38] Given the lack of evidence in the journals and the fact that Lewis was in camp that evening, we can only speculate about whether Clark

---

[38]Ibid., 4:219.

had his own espontoon or if he was using Lewis's. He had been a captain before leaving the army and may have had one from his previous service.

There is a last mention of Lewis's espontoon. Among the effects in his estate were "A Sword, Tomahawk, Pike blade & part of the Handle.[39] Almost certainly this was the one he had carried to the Pacific and back. It isn't surprising. Edged weapons like Lewis's espontoon or Sergeant Floyd's tomahawk are very personal. They are the type of things that a person kept or tried to return to families.

---

[39]Jackson, *Letters of the Lewis and Clark Expedition*, item 303:472.

CHAPTER 8

Ammunition

When Lewis and Clark readied the Corps of Discovery to leave St. Louis, they knew the Corps would be going into unknown country for an unknown period of time and recognized that the members of the expedition were going to have to feed themselves by hunting. Though the Corps was on a diplomatic mission, as well as one meant for exploration, it had to be prepared to defend itself.

The captains had made certain that there were plenty of firearms and brought the parts, tools, and an expert gunsmith needed to keep them working. It was also understood that powder and lead would be needed as gifts and trade goods. By the time they left St. Louis, Lewis and Clark had assured themselves that their supply of ammunition—several hundred pounds of powder and lead—was sufficient.

The ammunition the U.S. Army carried at the beginning of the nineteenth century was different from the ammunition it carries today. A round of ammunition for an M-16 consists of a bottle-necked cartridge of brass with an explosive cap in its base. It is filled with a smokeless powder and contains, like an extruded cork in the bottleneck, an aerodynamically modified cone of a bullet. The point of the bullet extends into the barrel of the rifle when the bullet is chambered. When the trigger releases the internal hammer, the hammer slams into the rear of a metal firing pin, which is driven into the cap at the base of the cartridge, causing it to explode and set off the powder in the cartridge. That explosion forces the bullet down the barrel

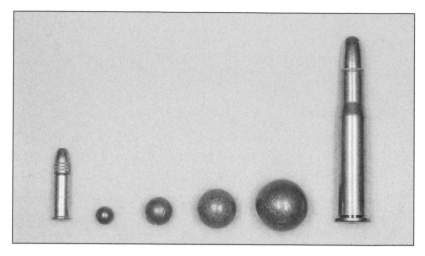

BALL SIZES

These are representative of the ball sizes the expedition carried. At the left end is a modern .22 caliber long rifle cartridge of today and at the right end a .30-.30 Winchester. The balls, left to right, are: buckshot, .36 caliber (similar to Clark's "small rifle"), .54 caliber (the size of a Harper's Ferry 1803 round), and .69 caliber (the bore diameter of the Model 1795 muskets). *Courtesy Michael F. Carrick.*

at speeds of 1,500 to 3,000 feet per second. The edges of the bullet, as they leave the chamber, are forced into the grooves of the rifling, preventing any gas from escaping around the bullet and imparting spin to it. Each of these self-contained cartridges is waterproof and safe to handle.

Two hundred years ago a "round" was literally that—a ball of lead—and a musket cartridge was a paper tube containing the ball and the powder needed to fire it. The ends of the tube were either folded or twisted to seal them. For a cartridge to be used, the end opposite the ball had to be bitten off and the powder dumped directly into the pan and barrel (see appendix B, "The Care and Feeding of the Flintlock," for more).

Most soldiers carried the ammunition for their muskets in cartridge boxes referred to as "cartouche" boxes, terminology the

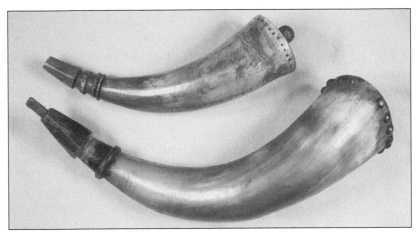

POWDER HORNS

These two horns—the size difference due to age and/or sex difference of the bovines—are characteristic of the types carried by expedition members. Smaller horns were often used for priming powder. The bases of the horns are sealed with wooden plugs held in place by tacks. The knob visible on base of the smaller horn could be used to attach one end of a shoulder strap while the other end could be attached around the grooves at the tip end. A stopper can be seen in the tip end of the larger horn. *Courtesy Michael F. Carrick.*

Americans picked up with the French weapons they fired during the Revolution. Most riflemen carried their powder in a horn or flask. They transported balls and other needed items in a bullet pouch, often referred to as a "possible sack," which was slung over the shoulder. Lewis withdrew fifteen powder horns and fifteen cartridge boxes from public stores and had fifteen bullet pouches made in Philadelphia. It is possible he also acquired an additional fifteen powder horns.

Cartridge boxes were leather, with a wooden block insert. The block had holes drilled in it to hold paper cartridges. The box was normally carried over the shoulder on a linen strap. A brush and pick were usually attached to the strap for quick access when cleaning the weapon's pan and touch hole was necessary. The powder horn generally had a measure attached that would hold the proper amount of powder to be introduced into the barrel. Rather than a cartridge box, the men usually carried a bullet pouch or possible sack, which would hold balls, patches, flints, tools, and more, plus the cleaning brush and pick if not attached to the shoulder strap. There was often a small knife for trimming the patches located in a handy place on the strap or in the pouch.

From the captains' journal entries, we know that the expedition had sufficient paper cartridges in midsummer 1805 to cache "one-half keg of fixed ammunition" below the Great Falls of the Missouri. Though the records are almost certainly incomplete, the Corps's ammunition supply at the beginning of the trip contained at least 401 pounds of powder, 840 pounds of lead, 650 gun flints, and some fabric unaccounted for in other uses, which could have been patch material for rifle ammunition. According to Lewis's equipment lists, the powder included 123 pounds of "English Canister Powder"; 53 pounds of the same in papers; 50 pounds of "best rifle powder" withdrawn from Harper's Ferry; and 175 pounds of powder supplied by Capt. Amos Stoddard while the Corps was at Camp Dubois (one 100-pound cask, and two acquisitions, one of 50 pounds and one of 25 pounds, in unspecified containers). Since it took a half-pound of powder to shoot a pound of lead, there should have been another 20 pounds of powder in the inventory, but there is no record of it. There were 52 lead canisters, which weighed a total of 416 pounds (round it off to 420 pounds), and 208 pounds of powder (say, 210 pounds). Unless some of the English powder in papers was unwrapped, these figures do not account for enough loose powder to have filled the 52 lead canisters. There may have been some powder unaccounted for in the records. Since there are so many references to amounts of powder that indicate a still-healthy supply late in the expedition, it seems likely that some records of acquisitions early in the trip are missing.

From Clark's journal entries we know that in addition to two muskets, the Corps cached a tin canister holding four pounds of powder, a keg of twenty pounds of powder, and an adequate proportion of lead at the mouth of the Marias River on June 9, 1805. This could account for some of the previously unrecorded powder. All the loose powder mentioned in the records came in weights of twenty-five, fifty, or one hundred pounds. The hundred-pound quantity was listed as being in a keg. None of the other units divide into four-pound units, and there is no previous mention of tin canisters. Seventeen days later, Lewis noted that they cached their two blunderbusses and one-half keg of fixed ammunition or, as Clark wrote, "catterages" (cartridges). It is not clear how one-half keg translates into weight or numbers of paper cartridges. If it is part of the fifty-three pounds in papers Lewis bought in Philadelphia, the half-keg would be twenty-six and a half pounds. Or this could as easily be some other unrecorded unit of ammunition.

Often a mention of ammunition in the journals only hints at how much and what type it was. These references frequently add to the confusion concerning how much ammunition the expedition members had and in what form it was packed.

Lewis apparently made the great innovation in packaging gunpowder—at least there is no record of anyone doing it before him. He recorded the innovation on August 6, 1805, relating that the expedition would have lost most of its powder to the wet except for "the expedient which I had fallen on of securing the powder by means of the lead having the latter formed into canesters which were filled with the necessary proportion of poder to discharge the lead when used, and those canesters which well secured with corks and wax." To this end, he had contracted with a Philadelphia plumber, George Ludlam, to make fifty-two lead canisters to hold gunpowder. Lewis's canisters weighed eight pounds and held four pounds of powder. The hole in the canister through which the powder was poured was sealed with a heavily waxed cork. These containers were mostly waterproof. As Clark recorded:

> Today we opened and examined all our Ammunition, which has been Secured in leaden Canistir.   we found twenty Sevin of the best

Rifle powder, 4 of the Common rifle, 3 Galize and one of Musquet powder in good order, perfectly as dry as when first put in the Canisters, although the whole of it from various accidence have been for hours under water.   these cannisters Contain 4 pounds of powder each and 8 of Lead.   had it not been for the hapy expedient which Capt Lewis devised of Securing the powder by means of the Lead, we Should have found great difficuelty in keeping dry powder untill this time—; those Cannisters which had been accidently brused and cracked, one which was carelessly Stoped, and a fifth which had penetrated with a nail; were wet and damaged; those we gave to the men to Dry; however exclusive of those 5 we have an abundant Stock to last us back.

Clark, February 1, 1806[1]

That "abundant Stock" amounted to 280 pounds of lead and 140 pounds of powder, which would be augmented by the cases at the Great Falls and at the mouth of the Marias, which amounted to another 24 pounds of powder, 48 pounds of lead, and half a keg of "fixed ammunition." The various calibers of weapons are not specified, but since they probably ranged from .35 to .50 caliber for the rifles and .63 caliber for the Model 1795 muskets, a conservative average of .50 caliber can be assumed, equaling 36 balls to the pound. So when the Corps was preparing to head back East, there was still the equivalent of more than 11,000 rounds, or enough for about 50 rounds per day. They had a sufficient supply to safely trade powder and lead for food and horses.

It is known that 420 pounds of lead were used in Lewis's canisters. Another 420 pounds was annotated as sheet lead. Yet, when Clark wrote of issuing ammunition during the preparation to leave Camp Dubois on May 10, 1804, he said, "order every man to have 100 balls for their Rifles & 2 lb. Of Buckshot for those with musquets."[2] So it is evident that the Corps was outfitted with buckshot as well as balls. The "Final Summation of Lewis' Account" shows that Lewis was reimbursed for a number of personal items, including a "fowling piece" that were "given in

---

[1]Moulton, *Journals of the Lewis and Clark Expedition*, 6:272.
[2]Ibid., 2:213.

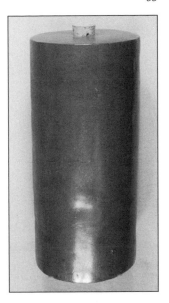

POWDER CANISTER

This is a replica of the canisters Lewis apparently invented. He had a Philadelphia plumber make them. They were lead, weighed eight pounds, and held four pounds of powder (the amount of powder that it took to fire that much lead). Once filled with powder, the hole in the top was stoppered with a cork and then the entire top sealed with wax. These were so waterproof that when checked at the mouth of the Columbia before heading back, they were all still dry on the inside. *Courtesy Michael F. Carrick.*

exchange for Canoe, Horses &c."[3] Since Lewis had a fowling piece, a shotgun, it seems reasonable to assume that there was birdshot as well. How much of either type of shot is not revealed in either the journals or the letters.

Aside from powder and lead, flintlock firearms needed flints. And not just any flints. A gun flint had to be properly constructed. When flints made their appearance in the sixteenth century, flint knapping, or shaping, technology was not new—the manufacturers were rediscovering Stone Age technology.[4] And the flint knappers' trade remained a craftsman trade; throughout the life of the flintlock, the flints were produced by hand. Gun flints were an important part of the firearms industry for over two centuries, until the caplock replaced the flintlock a generation or so after Lewis and Clark, and at the beginning of the nineteenth century, they were a major international trade item.

[3]Jackson, *Letters of the Lewis and Clark Expedition*, item 277:428.
[4]Peterson, *Encyclopedia of Firearms*, 146.

France and England were the two major suppliers, with France outstripping England, and at this time the flints the United States was using were largely imported.

Each gun flint would last for approximately 50 to 60 shots. Lewis had withdrawn "500 Best Rifle and 125 Musket" flints from public stores,[5] which would produce between 31,250 and 35,500 shots.[6] Since the expedition acquired more powder and lead on the frontier, it is not unreasonable to assume that Lewis and Clark must have procured the necessary number of flints as well. This would also explain the invoices prepared at Fort Mandan during the winter of 1804–1805 and sent back in the spring of 1805 with Corporal Warfington. These invoices state that after the expedition's first year the Corps had 925 gun flints left, which indicates that there were quite a few flints unaccounted for in the documents from the beginning of the journey, as Lewis had only recorded 625 coming from the East. Even if the men had brought 300 more with them, that doesn't account for all the target practice and shooting competitions at Camp Dubois and the hunting for food for over fifty men for over a year.

One-inch fabric patches were necessary to seat the balls properly in the rifle barrels; these could also be used as wadding when a musket or Lewis's fowling piece was loaded with buckshot or birdshot. One square yard of fabric would provide around 1,296 one-inch patches. Linen was considered excellent for patches, but any medium-weight, tightly woven fabric worked well. While in Philadelphia, in addition to the fabrics acquired for known uses, such as clothing, tenting, or for trade, Lewis purchased 32 yards of fine-milled cloth. Of the cloth, 28⅝ yards were used to make coats. The additional 3⅜ yards would have made excellent patch material. As the Corps wore out clothes, fabric would have been cannibalized for other uses, like patches. If no suitable fabric was available, pronghorn hides that were brain tanned (the Indian style of tanning), prepared by the men or traded for with Indians, would have made an excellent material for patching.

---

[5]Jackson, *Letters of the Lewis and Clark Expedition*, item 57:98.
[6]Peterson, *Encyclopedia of Firearms*, 146.

What use was made of all this ammunition? The only shot fired in anger was the one Lewis fired during the fight with the Blackfeet. At Camp Dubois, the Corps engaged in both target practice and in shooting competitions with locals. The target practice offered another way for the captains to evaluate the men's abilities, and the competitions forged *esprit*. The Corps may have fired volleys as part of the drills done to impress Missouri River tribes. There were salutes, with shoulder arms as well as blunderbusses and the swivel gun. But most of the ammunition used was for hunting, for gifts, and as a valuable trade item.

The journals contain no record of the Corps trading any ammunition in either 1803 or 1804, but in 1805 Clark traded one of the pistols along with a hundred balls and powder for a much-needed horse, which seems an appropriate trade. Until the first half of the expedition had been completed, the captains hadn't had a clear sense of the total amount of ammunition they needed, and this first gun and ammunition trade was for an item essential to completing their mission. On their return leg in 1806, they had a better idea of what they were likely to encounter, how much ammunition they would need, and hence how much they could use for trade. Fortunately for the Corps they had ammunition to spare, because they were almost out of other trade goods.

The captains recorded eleven trades or payments involving powder and lead as they headed home in 1806. All of these were important—securing horses, paying for the care of horses and gear left with the Nez Perces, or paying guides to help them across the Bitterroot Mountains. These transactions were significant enough that five guns were included in these payments. The amount of powder and lead involved cannot be exactly determined because some of the journal entries are for "a small amount" or "several hundred rounds," but judging from the trades for which the amounts are recorded, these involved a total of somewhere between a thousand and fifteen hundred rounds.

Once the Corps had returned to the Missouri, they seemed to be fully aware that they had more ammunition than they would need, and during the last six weeks of the journey, they made at least four gifts of ammunition. On August 12 they gave two trappers, Hancock and Dickson, two pounds of powder and "some" lead, and three days later, when John Colter was released from service to join those trappers, he was also given ammunition that Ordway hints was a two-year supply. Colter was one of the nine young men from Kentucky, so it is likely that he had his own rifle. If a two-year supply of ammunition comprises an average of one round per day (say .40 caliber, fifty-seven balls/lb.), then Colter was given at least the equivalent of 1½ of Lewis's lead canisters.

The Corps also gave the Mandan chief, Big White Chief, powder and lead. It is unclear whether the gift of the swivel gun to the Mandans included any ammunition for it. Additionally, they gave "a horn of powder and some balls" to two unnamed men they met on August 21, 1806.

There were small amounts of ammunition lost during the journey. On April 8, 1805, a boating accident resulted in thirty pounds of powder being soaked. Lewis lamented, "the powder we regard as a serious loss, but we spread it to dry immediately and hope we shall still be enabled to restore the greater part of it.   this was the only powder we had that was not perfectly secure from getting wet."[7] Three days later he added, "the powder which got wet by the same accedent and which we had spread to dry on the baggage of the large perogue, was now examined and put up; it appears to be almost restored, and our loss is therefore not so great as we had at first apprehended."[8] One month later, on May 14, a pirogue tipped and filled with water. Some items fell or floated from the boat, and Lewis wrote, on May 16, "the ballance of our losses consisted of some gardin seeds, a small quantity of gunpowder, and a few culinary articles which fell overboard and sunk."[9]

---

[7]Moulton, *Journals of the Lewis and Clark Expedition*, 4:13.
[8]Ibid., 4:22.
[9]Ibid., 4:156–57.

As mentioned above, Clark noted that five of the thirty-five lead canisters they still had at the end of their time at Fort Clatsop had leaked slightly. It is assumed that while at Fort Clatsop the damp powder would have needed to be dried inside, requiring a high degree of skill and care. During his exploration of the upper Mississippi at the same time as the Lewis and Clark Expedition, Zebulon Pike blew up part of his winter quarters in an attempt to dry wet gunpowder at an open fire. For Lewis and Clark, the only ammunition noted as lost during the return trip was George Shannon's powder horn and shot pouch, which he forgot to load into the canoe on September 13, less than two weeks from their arrival back in St. Louis. On the trip out, he would have been sent back for it, but that close to home, it was considered a loss and they went on. Even with a liberal assessment of how much ammunition the captains gave away, and considering the members of the Corps to be worse shots than the evidence indicates, the expedition still returned to St. Louis with at least half of the powder and lead that had been in the inventory when they left Fort Clatsop. The percentage remaining from the original ammunition inventory when the Corps left Camp Dubois in 1804 might have been enough to allow them to repeat their trip.

In spite of the wealth of ammunition carried by the Corps, the journals do record one instance of a depleted supply. George Shannon was lost for sixteen days in August and September of 1804. Upon rejoining the group on September 11, he reported that he had run out of ammunition twelve days earlier. Sergeant Ordway notes that Shannon had obtained at least one meal after running out of ball. Still having some powder left, he had substituted sticks for balls and had shot a rabbit. Invention is, indeed, the child of necessity.

CHAPTER 9

John Shields

On leaving St. Louis in the spring of 1804, the Corps of Discovery was as well armed as any expedition that headed into the West. The fact that it was still a superbly armed expedition on its return to St. Louis in the fall of 1806 is due to two things: Meriwether Lewis's excellent planning and John Shields's skills as a blacksmith and gunsmith. Lewis had the forethought not only to secure extra weapons but to bring along spare parts with which to make repairs. John Shields brought a gift for making and repairing things, often with a minimal tool kit. Lewis thought Shields had no formal training as a smith, writing:

> Shields renewed the main Spring of my air gun   we have been much indebted to the ingenuity of this man on many occasions; without having served any regular apprenticeship to any trade, he makes his own tools principally and works extreemly well in either wood or metal, and in this way has been extreemly serviceable to us, as well as being a good hunter and an excellent waterman.
>
> *Lewis, June 10, 1805*[1]

While he may have served no formal apprenticeship, Charles Clarke claims that John Shields ran a mill and blacksmith shop for his brother-in-law for at least part of the 1790s, and the fact that the captains gave him work as a blacksmith at Camp Dubois would seem to support this contention.[2] Alexander Willard was also assigned blacksmith work. Lewis's comments about the two

---

[1]Moulton, *Journals of the Lewis and Clark Expedition*, 4:275.
[2]Clarke, *The Men of the Lewis and Clark Expedition*, 53.

after the expedition, praising Shields but not Willard, and rec-
ommending Shields but not Willard, for extra pay because of his
splendid work, has caused many writers to speculate that Willard
worked as assistant to Shields. Lewis's detachment orders make
no such reference, though. The orders simply state that

> The Blacksmiths will also continue their work untill they have com-
> pleted the [articles?] contained in the memorandum with which I
> have furnished them, and during the time they are at work will recieve
> each an extra gill of whiskey pr. day and be exempt from guard duty;
> when the work is completed they will return to camp and do duty in
> common with the detatcment.
>
> *Lewis, February 20, 1804*[3]

John Shields's all-too-short biography in either Moulton or
Clarke tells us he was born near Harrisburg in Augusta County,
Virginia, one of twelve children born to Robert and Nancy
Stockton Shields. He was fifteen when the family moved to
Pidgeon Forge in Sevier County, Tennessee. Six years later he
married Nancy Wilson. After that Clarke says he worked for
Nancy's brother Samuel. Thirteen years later, still married and
the father of a daughter, Janette, Shields joined the Corps of
Discovery. One can only speculate on the reasons for his leaving
his family for three years to go West.

Shields's character begins to be revealed by the detachment
orders at the end of the winter of 1804. In orders on February
20, Lewis stated that in their absence the captains were leaving
Sergeant Ordway in charge. Orders from March 3 indicate that
things did not run smoothly during their absence.

> The Commanding officer feels himself mortifyed and disappointed at
> the disorderly conduct of Reubin Fields, in refusing to mount guard
> when in the due roteen of duty he was regularly warned; nor is he less
> surprised at the want of discretion in those who urged his oposition to
> the faithfull discharge of his duty, particularly Shields, whose sense
> of propryety he had every reason to beleive would have induced him
> reather to have promoted good order, than to have excited disorder

[3]Moulton, *Journals of the Lewis and Clark Expedition*, 2:175.

and faction among the party, particularly in the absence of Capt.
Clark and himself: The Commanding officer is also sorry to find any
man, who has been engaged by himself and Capt. Clark for the expedition on which they have entered, so destitute of understanding, as
not to be able to draw the distinction between being placed under the
command of another officer, whose will in such case would be their
law, and that of obeying the orders of Capt. Clark and himself com-
municated to them through Sergt. Ordway, who, as one of the party,
has during their necessary absence been charged with the execution
of their orders; acting from those orders expressly, and not from his
own capriece, and who, is in all respects accountable to us for the
faithfull observance of the same.

. . . The Carpenters Blacksmiths, and in short the whole party
(except Floid who has been specially directed to perform other duties)
are to obey implicitly the orders of Sergt. Ordway, who has received
our instructions on these subjects, and is held accountable to us for
their due execution.

M. Lewis Capt. March 3, 1804[4]

Unfortunately for history, the journals of the four men who were
present to view the situation—Ordway, Gass, Floyd, and Whitehouse—all begin on May 14, 1804, two and a half months after
the incident; there is little evidence of what exactly happened.
It does seem clear that Shields was singled out as having such
maturity that he should have helped resolve the situation as the
captains wanted, rather than adding to Sergeant Ordway's discipline problems.

This incident demonstrates the great difference between today's
United States Army and that of the early nineteenth century.
Basic training, as utilized in the modern military, molds soldiers.
At the beginning of the nineteenth century there was no separate
basic training program. While the men at Camp Dubois that
last week of February 1804 were all members of the Corps of
Discovery, a unit of the U.S. Army, only about half had been in
the army when they became part of the Corps. The other half
joined expressly for the expedition, and these men had been in
the army for as little as two months. They had spent virtually

---

[4]Ibid., 2:178–79.

all of that time preparing for the expedition, not in the drills that taught one how to be a soldier. Sergeant Ordway, on the other hand, was a regular, accustomed to receiving the respect accorded his rank and to having his orders carried out as if the captains were present.

To understand the quarrel between Ordway and his subordinates, triggered when Reuben Field refused an order to stand guard, a court-martial offense, it is important to try to understand the time and the people involved. Reuben Field was one of the nine young men from Kentucky, a frontiersman with a firm, instinctual grasp of certain aspects of his father's generation's revolutionary spirit. It is a spirit, a will, perhaps best expressed by a cowboy some eighty years later. A visiting English aristocrat asked the cowboy where the ranch owner was by saying, "I say, my good man, is your master about?" The cowboy replied, "The blankety-blank ain't been born yet." That attitude was one the U.S. army of the nineteenth century had trouble with on many occasions.

Reuben Field, a man who seems to have had what is often referred to as a practical turn of mind, may well have felt that common sense outweighed regulations, and that on that particular occasion, if not in the main, guard mount was unnecessary. John Ordway would have been of the opinion that regulations were to be followed—period. It is easy to imagine that the issue came to a head with neither man comprehending the other's position or even that there was another position. Ordway was a good sergeant. Reuben Field was a fire-eater. And that is a recipe for confrontation between two men with no "back down" in them.

Clearly, the men at Camp Dubois chose up sides, and the captains felt that rather than choosing sides, John Shields should have had the maturity to help resolve the quarrel. The question of his maturity had nothing to do with age, since Shields was only a couple of years older than Field. The captains had clearly seen something in Shields—common sense, competence, intelligence, solidity of character, or some combination of all—that caused them to instinctively put their trust in him. The journals indicate that this was the only occasion when he let them down.

The captains' journals are scanty for March of 1804, but the court-martial trial for the insurrection begun by Reuben Field wasn't held until the twenty-ninth, probably so that both of the captains could be present. There is no record of the punishment given, but it cannot have been too severe or have placed a serious black mark against any of the men, since all were assigned to the permanent party on the first of April and Reuben Field was sent out hunting the day after the trial. On March 30, Clark did note in his journal that "J. Sh: [Shields] & J. Co. [Colter] asked the forgivness & promised to doe better in future."[5] The fact that Shields never again caused trouble and that he performed his duties flawlessly points well to his maturity.

The captains' respect for and trust in Shields was based on his work more than any other outward manifestations of maturity. That trust was indicated in Lewis's "roll of the men who accompanied me on my late tour to the Pacific Ocean. . ." submitted to Secretary of War Henry Dearborn:

18. John Shields Private	Has received the pay only of a private. Nothing was more peculiarly useful to us in various situations, than the skill and ingenuity of this man as an artist, in repairing our guns, accoutrements, &c. and should it be thought proper to allow him something as an artificer, he has well deserved it.

Shields received, as did all the members of the Permanent Party, double pay and a land grant of 320 acres.[6]

The captains' obvious trust in and respect for him raises questions. His maturity and talents would seem to have qualified him as a sergeant, yet there is no evidence that promoting him was ever considered. If he was illiterate, he would have been

---

[5]Ibid., 2:183.
[6]Jackson, *Letters of the Lewis and Clark Expedition*, item 236:367.

disqualified, since sergeants needed to be able to read written orders and to keep unit records, but there is no evidence of his literacy or the lack thereof. It seems more likely that the captains wanted him free to work as a smith. The request for additional pay shows how valuable he was to the expedition, and had the Army of 1800 been organized as it is today, perhaps he would have been made a warrant officer.

There is also evidence that Shields participated in the scientific branch of the expedition. He brought Lewis several animal type specimens to measure and record. Since a type specimen is the first recorded example of a species, any hunter might be expected to shoot and bring to Lewis any animal he hadn't seen before. But Shields brought in plant and geological specimens as well, indicating a real interest in the expedition's scientific work.

Though the journals reveal Shields to be a competent hunter, his real value in procuring food for the Corps was by fabricating trade goods. That ability was most obvious during the winter of 1804–1805 while wintering at Fort Mandan. Aside from selling off sheet iron from a worn-out stove (Shield received seven or eight gallons of corn for a four-inch square of iron), he and Willard were paid well for making many items for the Mandans, in particular ax heads.

> visited by many of the natives who brought a considerable quantity of corn in payment for the work which the blacksmith had done for them—   they are pecuarly attached to a *battle ax* formed in a very inconvenient manner in my opinion.   it is fabricated of iron only, the blade is extremely thin, from 7 to nine inches in length and from 4¾, to 6 Inches on it's edge, from whence the sides proceed nearly in a straight line to the eye where it's width is generally not more than an inch. The eye is round & about one inch in diameter.   the handle seldom more than fourteen inches in length, the whole weighing about one pound-the great length of the blade of this axe, added to the small size of the handle renders a stroke uncertain and easily avoided, while the shortness of the handel must render a blow much less forceable if even well directed, and still more inconvenient as they uniformally use this instrument in action on horseback. The oalder fassion is still more inconvenient, it is somewhat in the form

of the blade of an Espantoon but is attached to a helve of the demen-
tions before discribed   the blade is sometimes by way of ornament
purforated with two or more small circular holes—

Lewis, February 5, 1805[7]

Lewis concluded the next day with

the blacksmith's have proved a happy resoce to us in our present situation as I believe it would have been difficult to have devised any
other method to have procured corn from the natives.

Lewis, February 6, 1805[8]

This was the last time the plural "blacksmiths" is used. After
the winter at Fort Mandan, Alexander Willard is never again
mentioned as a smith; from then on Shields seems to have done
all the blacksmithing and gunsmithing by himself, and during
the first half of the trip, he certainly had the tools as well as the
skills. Besides his blacksmith's forge, he was well supplied with
all the tools and spare parts he needed to keep the weapons in
working order. On leaving Fort Mandan, the journals reveal
fifteen spare gun locks as well as tools.

The Corps of Discovery reached the mouth of the Marias River
the first week of June 1805. Knowing they were approaching the
Great Falls of the Missouri, past which they would not be able
to take their pirogues, they prepared to cache materials they
wouldn't be able to carry. Caches were dug between the mouth
of the Marias and Great Falls. Some things were abandoned
because of space limitations and difficulty of portaging; others
they felt could be spared at the time but might be needed on the
return trip. The pirogues were cached because they couldn't be
portaged and couldn't be used in the smaller waters upstream.
Shields's forge was placed in the cache at the mouth of the
Marias. As Lewis wrote,

and, as we had determined to leave our blacksmith's bellows and tools
here it was necessary to repare some of our arms, and particularly
my Airgun the main spring of which was broken, before we left this

---

[7]Moulton, *Journals of the Lewis and Clark Expedition*, 3:286–87.
[8]Ibid., 3:288.

place.   these and other preparations will necessarily detain us two or perhaps three days.

Lewis, June 9, 1805[9]

Clark's journal entry for June 11 indicates that Shields didn't complete his work until too late on that day to commence traveling. From there on, Shields's work as a blacksmith and gunsmith was done with a very minimal tool kit.

Shields's work with that kit began a week later, when he was called on to build a replacement for a missing screw from the kit to assemble the iron-frame boat. This boat, designed by Lewis and built to his specifications at Harper's Ferry, was thirty-two feet long and was intended to serve as a replacement for a pirogue. The captains' faith in Shields is clearly stated by Lewis: "examined the frame of my Iron boat and found all the parts complete except one screw, which the ingenuity of Shields can readily replace, a resource which we have very frequent occasion for."[10] From that day, June 18, until Lewis finally gave up on July 9, he tried to cover the boat frame with hides, as was called for in the design. Unfortunately, there were no conifer trees near the Great Falls and hence no pitch with which to seal the seams. Without seam sealant, the boat leaked too badly to be used, so it was cached and never retrieved. And from this point until the expedition's time at Fort Clatsop, there is no evidence of Shields serving as a blacksmith.

One month after the abandonment of the iron-framed boat at the Great Falls, with the Jefferson River becoming smaller and more tightly wound, Lewis set out ahead of the main party to search for the Shoshones. He took Shields, Hugh McNeal, and George Drouillard with him. On this scouting trip Lewis recorded his second and last disappointment with Shields. The party was crossing Horse Prairie, McNeal with Lewis and Drouillard and Shields on the flanks, when they encountered a young Shoshone who was horseback. Lewis described the incident.

---

[9]Ibid., 4:271.
[10]Ibid., 4:306.

I now sent Drewyer to keep near the creek on my right and Shields to my left, with orders to surch for the road which if they found they were to notify me by placing a hat in the muzzle of their gun. I kept McNeal with me; after having marched in this order for about five miles I discovered an Indian on horse back about two miles distant coming down the plain toward us. with my glass I discovered from his dress that he was of a different nation from any that we had yet seen, and was satisfyed of his being a Sosone; his arms were a bow and quiver of arrows, and was mounted on an eligant horse without a saddle, and a small string which was attached to the underjaw of the horse which answered as a bridle. I was overjoyed at the sight of this stranger and had no doubt of obtaining a friendly introduction to his nation provided I could get near enough to him to convince him of our being whitemen.   I therefore proceeded towards him at my usual pace. When I had arrived within about a mile he mad a halt which I did also. . . I mad him the signal of friendship. . . he kept his position and seemed to view Drewyer or Shields who were now comiming in sight on either hand with an air of suspicion. . . I therefore haistened to take out of my sack some b[e]ads a looking glas and a few trinkets which I had brought with me for this purpose and leaving my gun and pouch with McNeal advanced unarmed towards him.   he remained in the same steadfast poisture untill I arrived in about 200 paces of him when he turn his horse about and began to move off slowly from me; I now called to him in as loud a voice as I could command repeating the *tab-ba-bone*, which in their language signifyes *white man*.   but loking over his shoulder he still kept his eye on Drewyer and Shields who wer still advancing neither of them having segacity enough to recollect the impropriety of advancing when they saw me thus in parley with the Indian. I now made a signal to these men to halt, Drewyer obeyed but Shields who afterwards told me he did not observe the signal still kept on the Indian halted again and turned his ho[r]se about as if to wait for me, and I believe he would have remained untill I came up whith him had it not been for Shields who still pressed forward. whe I arrived with about 150 paces I again repeated the word tab-ba-bone and held up the trinkets in my hands and striped up my shirt sleeve to give him the opportunity of seeing the colour of my skin and advanced leasure towards him but he did not remain untill I got nearer than about 100 paces when he suddonly turned his ho[r]se about, gave him the whip leaped the creek and disapeared in the willow brush in an instant. . . I felt soarly chargrined at the conduct of the men particularly Shields to whom I principally attributed this failure in obtaining an introduction to the natives. I now called the men to me and could not forbare abraiding them a little for their want of attention and imprudence on this occasion.

Lewis, August 11, 1805[11]

Since the party successfully met the Shoshones two days later, all seems to have been forgiven. The next time there was a need for an advance party, Clark chose Shields to be one of the six hunters to accompany him to rush through the Bitterroots in search of food. The food they found was with the Nez Perces, who shared not only their food but their knowledge of the country. Leaving the Nez Perces, the expedition headed downstream for the Pacific in newly built canoes with newly acquired maps.

Between leaving the Nez Perces in October 1805 and arriving at the Pacific in November, John Shields's duties were routine. While the Corps was in a temporary camp on the north side of the mouth of the Columbia, Shields took part in what was certainly one of the more interesting votes in the nineteenth century. On November 24 the entire party voted to decide where to spend the winter. It was a vote that was 120 years ahead of its time, since everyone, including York and Sacagawea, had a vote. Shields was the only one whose clear preference was to head back immediately. He voted to return to and winter at the mouth of the Sandy River, which drains into the Columbia from the slopes of Mount Hood. There is no indication of why Shields felt that way. It should also be noted that when, one week earlier, Clark offered to take everyone who wanted to go for a better view of the ocean, Shields showed no interest.

Once Fort Clatsop was built and occupied, Lewis wrote the last recorded detachment order on January 1, 1806, setting out the rules for the winter. The order covered the use of tools. Everyone except Shields was required to return any tools "the moment he has ceased to use them." Shields's exception was duly noted as well: "the tools loaned to John Shields are excepted from the restrictions of this order."[12] That seems to make clear not only

---

[11]Ibid., 5:68–70.
[12]Ibid., 6:158.

the trust the captains had in their blacksmith but the fact that he was engaged in fabrication and repair work through the winter. As the winter stay neared its end,

the guns of Drewyer and Sergt. Pryor were both out of order. the first was repared with a new lock, the old one having become unfit for uce; the second had the cock screw broken which was replaced by a duplicate which had been prepared for the lock at Harper's ferry where she was manufactured. but for the precaution taken in bringing on those extra locks, and parts of locks, in addition to the ingenuity of John Shields, most of our guns would at this moment be untirely unfit for use; but fortunately for us I have it in my power here to record that they are all in good order.

Lewis, March 20, 1806[13]

The winter at Fort Clatsop was a hardship for the entire party. Not only was it constantly cold, wet, and damp, but food was scarce. The men were living on elk and the little bit of other foods available through trade with Indians who were accustomed to trade, but not overimpressed with the Corps's meager supply of trade goods. On at least one occasion gunsmithing services obtained some food. Clark described that on the last day of 1805, "a *Skil lute* brought a gun which he requested me to have repaired, it only wanted a Screw flattened So as to catch, I put a flint into his gun& he presented me in return a peck of *Wappato* for payment."[14] I have found no other notes on such similar transactions and no mention of John Shields doing work similar to what he did at Fort Mandan. That raises the question of whether his services weren't called for or whether his lack of the forge he'd had the winter before prevented him from setting up a shop that might have been most beneficial to the Corps's trade relations with the surrounding population. The incident also indicates that, though Shields was the expedition gunsmith, at least some of the men were competent to recognize problems and do minor repair work themselves. The many references to Shields being called on to work on weapons would point to the

---

[13]Ibid., 6:441.
[14]Ibid., 6:147.

very hard usage and rugged conditions to which the weapons were subject.

John Shields was not simply working as a blacksmith and hunter. He made a set of elk-skin bags designed to hold Clark's papers and various articles that he wished to keep dry. Shields's hunting time was devoted to science as well as elk. For instance, he was part of the group that went to see the remains of a dead whale that had washed up on the beach in the winter of 1805–1806, and he, along with Reuben Field and Robert Frasure (Frazer), measured what Clark recorded as "2 trees of the fur kind one 37 feet around, appears sound, has fiew limbs for 200 feet. . . abt 280 feet high."[15] There is evidence that Shields's scientific curiosity was not something he had acquired from the captains, for it was Shields who finally suggested the cure for William Bratton's mysterious back ailment that plagued him from the end of the Fort Clatsop winter until the Corps's time at Camp Chopunnish, their long camp on the Clearwater River. As Lewis recorded on May 24, 1806, "John Shields observed that he had seen men in a similar situation restored by violent sweats."[16] Shields even had a specific tea to administer with the sweat. Bratton was cured.

On April 7, 1806, Clark recorded, "We made our men exersise themselves in Shooting and regulateing their guns, found Several of them that had their Sights moved by accident, and others that wanted Some little alterations all which were compleated rectified in the Course of the day except my Small rifle, which I found wanted Cutting out." This was Clark's relatively small bored Pennsylvania-style rifle. Excessively firing had worn the barrel so much that the rifling was no longer deep enough to grip the patched ball properly, making the ball lose the spin necessary to impart accuracy. Cutting out the barrel meant deepening the grooves of the rifling, a job normally done in a well-equipped gun shop. Though most of his smithing tools were in the cache at the mouth of the Marias, Shields was still up to the task. Clark's

[15]Ibid., 6:390.
[16]Ibid., 7:283.

journal entry continues with "John Shields Cut out my Small rifle & brought hir to Shoot very well.   the party ows much to the injenuity of this man, by whome their guns are repared when they get out of order which is very often."[17] This job as much as any indicates not only Shields's skill but his ingenuity in performing such a job with such a minimal tool kit.

At the beginning of July, 1806, as the captains prepared to split the expedition so they could explore the overland route to the Great Falls, the Marias, and the Yellowstone, Shields spent two days refurbishing the Corps's firearms.

> had all of our arms put in the most prime order   two of the rifles have unfortunately bursted near the muscle, Shields Cut them off and they Shute tolerable well   one which is very Short we exchanged with the Indian who we had given a longer gun to induc them to pilot us across the Mountains.
>
> *Clark, July 2, 1806*[18]

There is no indication of whether or not Shields put new front sights on the rifles, though the "tolerable well" suggests that he might have.

John Shields accompanied Clark on his exploration of the Yellowstone. Clark's journal indicates that he had Shields out hunting much of the time but also had him check the temperature of the hot springs in Jackson, Montana, by cooking meat in the two pools. He also trusted Shields, as they traveled down the Yellowstone, to search for trees suitable for canoes, writing on July 20, 1806, "I directed Sergt. Pryor and Shields each of them good judges of timber to proceed on down the river Six or 8 miles and examine the bottoms if any larger trees . . . can be found."[19] He also asked Shields to search for wild ginger to use as a poultice for George Gibson's leg wound. Gibson had fallen on a log and stuck a stob into his thigh. This indicates that Shields had knowledge of wild plants.

---

[17]Ibid., 7:95.
[18]Ibid., 8:80.
[19]Ibid., 8:208.

Coupled with his knowing about sweat baths and accompanying teas, the knowledge of plants indicates a part of Shields's character that has never been explored, and probably can't be, given the lack of written records.

Since the Corps's weapons were put to hard daily use and the flintlock was an inherently delicate piece of equipment, Shields may be regarded as one of the main reasons the Corps didn't starve to death. That, coupled with his overall performance, seems to explain why it was that at the end of the trip Lewis thought enough of Shields and the service he gave to the Corps of Discovery that he recommended that Shields be given a monetary bonus in addition to the land bonus all Corps members were to receive.

After the Corps's return to St. Louis, our knowledge of Shields's life is sketchy at best.

Moulton says that he stayed in Missouri for a time, trapping and hunting with Daniel Boone, a kinsman, before settling in Indiana, where he died in 1809, just three years after the expedition's return. He was only forty years old at his death. His life leaves that lingering, not quite identifiable aftertaste in a historian's mouth; not all of the ingredients are listed in the recipe. It seems hardly enough to know that the Corps of Discovery would have been sans guns without him.

CHAPTER 10

The Gun Trade

O nce the Corps of Discovery crossed the Continental Divide, the Corps met tribes that had never seen white men. But it never met a tribe that had not traded for white men's goods. In fact, it never contacted people who did not have at least some firearms. During the return trip, that fact became of critical importance to the Corps's survival because the tribes were as American as Lewis and Clark: they never had enough guns and ammunition.

The Corps was short on trade goods. As it prepared to leave Fort Clatsop, Lewis noted in his journal that

> two handkercheifs would now contain all the small articles of mer-
> chandize which we possess; the ballance of the stock consists of 6
> blue robes one scarlet do.   One uniform artillerist's coat and hat,
> five robes made of our large flag, and a few old cloaths trimed with
> ribbon.   on this stock we have wholy to depend for the purchase
> of horses and such portion of our subsistence from the Indians as it
> will be in our powers to obtain.   a scant dependence indeed, for a
> tour of the distance of that before us.
>
> Lewis, March 16, 1806[1]

Guns and ammunition, especially ammunition, made up the deficit. Guns, if properly cared for lasted for years. Ammunition was an expendable good that had to be replaced as it was used up. For tribes without regular contact with white traders, ammunition was a very valuable trade item. As noted in the chapter on ammunition, the Corps of Discovery had more than enough

---

[1]Moulton, *Journals of the Lewis and Clark Expedition*, 6:421.

ammunition to meet its own needs. Therefore, though Lewis seemingly did not realize this in the spring of 1806, it was well supplied with trade goods of the first order, powder and lead.

How had tribes so remote from white sources of firearms acquired these weapons? There were several main sources of guns for these peoples. First, the route the expedition followed up the Missouri to the Mandan Nation was a major trade area, and guns were certainly part of that trade. The second source was the Northern Plains trading spheres of the Hudson Bay Company (HBC), founded in 1670, and the Northwest Company, founded in 1783 in direct, intentional competition with the HBC. These two companies were in a trade war that at times included shooting and that lasted from 1783 until the HBC bought out the Northwesters in 1820. The HBC and Northwest traders, and their Indian trading allies, were located throughout the upper Missouri and northern plains areas, and the firearms moving into the southern plains from the lower Mississippi and New Mexico areas were traded north to the Mandan areas as well. Once beyond the Rockies the Corps was in an overlap trade area. HBC and the Northwest goods moved in from the north and east, and the Pacific Northwest coastal trade goods found their way up the Columbia.

Virtually all of this trade was conducted by tribal middle-men. On the coast, where the Corps was amazed at the Indians' knowledge of the value of trade goods, the expedition encoun-tered tribes who had become knowledgeable traders because of their direct contact with the white coastal trade. In 1805, before the arrival of Lewis and Clark, 13 ships involved in the Pacific Northwest trade had passed the mouth of the Columbia River, and of the 15 American ships that passed the river's mouth in the spring of 1806, none arrived before the expedition headed back East. Those 28 ships had been preceded by 213 vessels since the British ship the *Sea Otter* had come up the coast in 1785. In other words, the folks around the mouth of the Columbia had two decades of exposure to European trade and trade goods—more than enough time to be aware of the quality and value of various goods. That put the expedition in hard straits since it had few things left to trade. Or, as Clark put it on November 24, 1805, "we have every reason to believe that the nativs have not provisions Sufficent for our Consumption, and if they had, their prices are So high that it would take ten times as much to purchase their roots & Dried fish as we have in our possession."[2] So the Corps fell back on its guns and the men relied on hunting elk to feed themselves through the winter. It was less than two months later that Lewis had reason to write "most of the party have become very expert with the rifle."[3]

The vessels of the Pacific Northwest fur trade had probably not sharpened the trading skills of the coast tribes. Trade was ancient, and trade routes had spread from the Pacific coast to the Great Plains long before Leif Ericson, let alone Columbus. But those American and European vessels had exposed the tribes to white goods, so that Lewis and Clark found not only sophisticated traders but ones who knew the value of European and American goods. One thing the expedition members found in some abundance was firearms. On November 17, 1805, Clark wrote, "the name of the nation is <Chin-noo> Chinook and is noumerous   live principally on fish roots a fiew Elk and fowls.   they are well armed with good Fusees."[4] On January 9, 1806, Lewis described the view of the Northwest coastal fur trade: "This traffic on the part of the whites consists in vending guns, (principally old british or American musquits) powder, balls and Shot."[5]

The problem Indians encountered was not in obtaining firearms but in maintaining them. The Corps was able to trade gunsmithing services for a peck of Clatsop-prepared wapato roots on at least one occasion. That problem of maintaining firearms seldom kept men who could afford one from purchasing

---

[2]Ibid., 6:85.
[3]Ibid., 6:224.
[4]Ibid., 6:60.
[5]Ibid., 6:187.

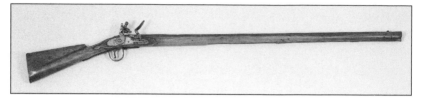

TRADE GUN

Trading with the Indians had from its early days included firearms. Guns of this and similar designs were an important part of the trade from the mid-eighteenth to the mid-nineteenth century. The expedition took no guns specifically for trading. *Courtesy Buffalo Bill Historical Center, Cody, Wyoming, U.S.A.; Gift of Olin Corporation, Winchester Arms Collection, 1988.8.1328.*

a gun—and the traders knew that. When the *Atahualpa* sailed from Boston to the Northwest coast in 1801, James R. Gibson notes that its trade goods included "3000 unknown units of gun powder, 250 leather [powder] flasks, 150 cartouche boxes, 350 muskets, 20 pistols." He then noted that in 1806 the seasoned trader William Sturgis recommended that "Muskets need not be sent unless the best kind King's arms can be procur'd & then not more than 100 would sell—BB & mould Shott, say one Ton & Two of Bar Lead—Brass blunderbusses will sell well—Pistols do not answer." Later Sturgis, talking about what trade goods were wanted, was specific: "muskets (particularly Speak rather than French or Kendrick muskets)."[6] In other words, at the time of the expedition, firearms were common enough for traders to be conscious that they needed specific types and makes of weapons. Since firearms were not yet universal, they served

[6]Gibson, *Otter Skins, Boston Ships and China Goods,* 214–24. An interesting footnote to what was demanded during the trade in flintlocks in the West is that gun flints were included in the lists of goods of most of the Indian traders at the time of Lewis and Clark. For reasons that say volumes about human nature, tribes who were still primarily equipped with worked stone implements—people who were some of the finest flint knappers in the world—traded for gun flints. When we acquire a new technology, we want to acquire it as a package.

not only as weapons for war and tools for hunting but as status symbols as well.

The gun trade dealt almost exclusively in trade muskets, muskets and fusils designed specifically for the Indian trade. It is often stated that these were inferior weapons made to sell more than to use. But within a very short time Indians were demanding guns that worked and worked well. So it was that the Clatsops, who were quite knowledgeable about muskets, were not familiar with rifles.

after amuseing my Self for about an hour on the edge of the rageing Seas I returned to the houses, one of the Indians pointed to a flock of Brant Sitting in the creek at Short distance below and requested me to Shute one, I walked down with my Small rifle and killed two at about 40 yds distance, on my return to the houses two Small ducks Set at about 30 steps from me the Indians pointed at the ducks they were near together, I Shot at the ducks and accidently Shot the head of one off, this Duck and brant was Carried to the house and every man Came around and examined the Duck looked at the gun the Size of the ball which was 100 to the pound and Said in their language *Clough Musket* [NB: English word Musket][7] *wake, com ma-tax Musket* which is, a good Musket do not under Stand this kind of Musket &c.

Clark, December 10, 1805[8]

Clark is not clear about whether the Clatsop mystification is with the small caliber (a hundred balls to the pound is .36 caliber, while their muskets and fusils were probably a minimum of .50 caliber), with the rifling or both. It is possible that none of them had seen a rifle before. And if one forgets to mention that shooting the head off a duck was an accident, it is an impressive shot. Most men would assume your gun was more accurate, not that you were a better shot.

There were multiple reasons to use smooth-bored weapons in the Indian trade. But the most likely was that smooth-bored

---

[7] This comment designated [NB:] is, to quote Moulton, "Nicholas Biddle's emendations or interlineations." *Journals of the Lewis & Clark Expedition.*

[8] Moulton, *Journals of the Lewis and Clark Expedition*, 6:121.

weapons are much cheaper to make than rifles, since there is both less metal in, and less tooling of, the barrels.

Though the Indians along the Pacific coast had more contact with white traders and hence more access to guns and metal goods, ironware and weapons had spread along at least the major trade routes the Corps of Discovery followed. Guns moved up the Columbia and Snake Rivers from the coast, down out of Canada via trade with HBC and the Northwest Company, up the Missouri with French and American traders, and up from the southern plains, primarily from the lower Mississippi Valley. Everywhere Lewis and Clark went they found Indians possessing guns. That fact made their return trip considerably easier, since they could often trade ammunition for needed goods. Eleven times the expedition was able to use ammunition alone to pay for goods and services ranging from horses to the Nez Perces' caring for their horses and cached goods. This fact, more than the scattered references to Indian firearms, suggests that guns were present even in the areas most removed from direct white contact, along the upper reaches of the Columbia and Missouri drainages.

These facts reveal two important aspects of the history of the area. First, the whites had simply plugged themselves into existing trade networks. For instance, the Nez Perces, according to Alan Pinkham, one of the tribe's historians, traded from the Pacific to central Montana and from the Four Corners area to Slave Lake.[9] That is a huge trading area but not an unusual one for a tribe located, as the Nez Perces were, at a crossroads. They were at one of the headwaters of the Columbia River system and had for countless generations trekked over the same trail Lewis and Clark followed through the Bitterroot Mountains, to trade and to hunt on the plains of Montana. They had carried sea shells to the Crows and buffalo robes to the trade fair at Celilo Falls on the Columbia from time out of mind, and they were not unique in their trading ventures. What the white traders had done was to introduce new goods into long-established

---

[9]Personal conversation with author.

trade networks, thus integrating the tribes of the American West into the worldwide trading system and introducing them to the Europeans and Americans who were coming into their world.

The captains' seeming insistence on taking all the powder and lead they could lay their hands on proved to be a great help. Not only was the expedition assured of being able to hunt, and to defend itself if necessary, it was even able to cache weapons and ammunition against disaster. And without those weapons and ammunition to trade, the Corps may well have been left afoot, unable to complete its assignment or even to survive. And that was only possible because the gun trade was already well established throughout their area of travel.

Conclusions

On August 11, 1806, between the mouth of the Yellowstone and the Mandan Villages, Clark's contingent of the Corps of Discovery met Joseph Dickson and Forest Hancock, two trappers and traders from Illinois who were the first of the wave of white men headed to the upper Missouri seeking the soft gold of western furs. The Corps's own reconnaissance was winding down. Below the mouth of the Yellowstone was country already surveyed, so its work was essentially done.

The Corps spent four days with the Mandans for the sake of diplomacy, to settle some accounts with them and with the Charbonneaus, and to discharge John Colter, who wanted to stay in the West with Dickson and Hancock, who had come back to the Mandan area. From there it took just over a month to cover the distance it had taken them almost eight months to cover in 1804. Not all of that speed was due to working with rather than against the current. There was little scientific research and mapmaking to do on this stretch, and it seems certain that the men felt they were finished with the voyage's important work. Once past the Teton Sioux, the Corps's guns became nothing more than tools to feed themselves—until they reached civilization.

On September 6, 1806, they met one of René Auguste Chouteau's trading boats headed up the Missouri to trade with the Yanktons. The captains

> purchased a gallon of whiskey of this man [NB: promised to pay Coteau who would not receive any pay][1] and gave to each man of the party a

---

[1] The comments designated [NB:] are, to quote Moulton, "Nicholas Biddle's emendations or interlineations." *Journals of the Lewis & Clark Expedition.*

dram which is the first Spiritious licquor which had been tasted by any of them Since the 4 of July 1805.   Several of the party   exchanged leather for linen Shirts and beaver for Corse hats.

Clark, September 6, 1806[2]

Either Clark had forgotten it or did not consider John Collins's beer, apparently made from camas roots, to be spirituous liquor, though at the time (October 21, 1805) all thought it acceptable. A week and a half after meeting the trading boat, they traded Mandan corn for "Buisquit, Chocolate Sugar & whiskey"[3] with Captain McClellin, a recently discharged friend of Lewis's who was headed upriver on a trading venture. These were but brushes with the fringes of civilization now extending up the river; it was another two weeks to the first settlement. There, attired as citizens rather than as wild men and with at least a fresh memory of the taste of civilization on their tongues, the men of the Corps, bred to the frontier and two years beyond its borders, demonstrated the gun's use as a celebratory tool on their return:

> the party being extreemly anxious to get down ply their ores very well, we Saw Some cows on the bank which was a joyfull Sight to the party and Caused a Shout to be raised for joy   at [blank] PM we Came in Sight of the little french Village called Charriton [NB: Chartette]   the men raised a Shout and Sprung upon their ores and we soon landed opposit to the Village.   our party requested to be permited to fire off their Guns which was alowed & they discharged 3 rounds with a harty Cheer.

Clark, September 20, 1806[4]

Three more days and the Corps of Discovery was back in St. Louis. The swivel gun that had saluted their departure from Camp Dubois just over twenty-eight months before was now the property of the Mandans. But the return demanded a proper salute. And a proper salute meant guns.

> decended to the Mississippi and down that river to St. Louis at which place we arived about 12 oClock.   we Suffered the party to   fire

---

[2]Moulton, *Journals of the Lewis and Clark Expedition*, 8:351.
[3]Ibid., 8:363.
[4]Ibid., 8:367.

off their pieces as a Salute to the Town.   we were met by all
the   village and received a harty welcom from it's inhabitants &c.

Clark, September 23, 1806[5]

The Corps of Discovery was dispersed at St. Louis, though
Lewis and Clark still had months of work and further travel to
Washington before the expedition was officially finished.

Not only were the members of the Corps dispersed, the equipment was too. The notes of Lewis's accounts state:

Meriwether Lewis Captn. 1 Regt. Infty. Dr. To Expedition to the
Pacific Ocean.   For so much received by him, being the net
proceeds of   the sale of Sundry Rifles, Muskets, powder horns,
Shot pouches, Powder, Lead, Kettles, Axes, & other public property
remaining on hand at the   termination of the Expedition to the
Pacific Ocean, which were disposed of at public Auction at St. Louis
pr.   a/c   408.62[6]

That sale ends the traceable history of the Corps's weapons. Government weapons were sold, perhaps to men who were themselves
headed into the West. The men dispersed, taking their personal
gear with them. All the permanent party members were not only
paid their wages but were given land grants as a bonus. Some
settled down to farm, some returned to the East. Sergeant Gass
stayed in the Army until an injury blinded him in one eye. George
Drouillard and John Potts returned to the Rocky Mountains
the next year and were both killed, in separate incidents, at the
Three Forks of the Missouri. Clark who, had his education been
more classical, might have quoted the St. Crispin's Day speech
from *Henry V* to the men as they swept down the last mile to St.
Louis, kept track of the men the rest of his life, and in the 1820s
he recorded where everyone was or what had happened to him.

But quickly enough all the men passed from the public con-
sciousness and the expedition passed into history. While the
journals were eventually published and maps were produced,
probably the most useful information in the short run stayed

---

[5]Ibid., 8:370.
[6]Jackson, *Letters of the Lewis and Clark Expedition*, item 277:424.

in the oral tradition of those members of the Corps who stayed along the frontier or returned to the West. And the tribes who met the Corps talked about and contemplated the wave of whites that the Corps foretold. Their oral traditions kept their histories until replaced in modern times by their own written histories and today's computer files.

When histories are passed on, written or told, there is a question that must be asked, and often is asked, by children forced to read or listen: So what? The answer to that should be on more than one level. Is it a good story? Yes, the Corps of Discovery's tale is one of epic proportions. Can new writing answer questions not yet covered, and can new work correct mistakes in older writings and research? This book has attempted to do some of that. For instance, Gary Moulton's wonderful edition of the Corps's journals relied on Carl P. Russell's *Guns of the Early Frontiers: A History of Firearms from Colonial Times through the Years of the Western Fur Trade* and his *Firearms, Traps, and Tools of the Mountain Men*, books that have been the standard references for over forty years. Over those decades, much research has been done not only on the Corps of Discovery but on the weaponry of the period. So there are corrections that need to be gathered together. For instance, Russell assumed Lewis had been able to get Harper's Ferry Model 1803 Rifles, a conclusion based on the almost total lack of published research on the Harper's Ferry Arsenal when Russell was writing.

Lewis and Clark's weapons were tools. Hopefully, this book is also a tool, one that will help put the expedition, and the history of the white exploration and settlement of the West, in clearer context. The tale of the Corps of Discovery is but a small piece of the story of who the American people want to be, the story we call the American Myth, a story that is but a small piece of the European explosion across the globe. . . . As William Clark would write, "&c. &c."

Read on, extensively. May all your travels, in libraries and on the road, be like those of the Corps of Discovery and all the peoples they met, voyages of discovery.

Who Carried What

B est evidence suggests there were fifty-four members of the expedition, from the captains to the engagés, who might have carried firearms. Lewis and Clark each wrote about their personal rifles. In all probability, York, Clark's lifelong hunting companion, had his own gun. We know that at least seventeen of the men came from military units and probably brought Model 1795 muskets with them, and it seems likely that the nine young men from Kentucky brought their personal rifles. Drouillard also certainly and Charbonneau quite likely had their own weapons. And there are twenty-one men for whom there is not even a good guess. In other words, with ten volumes of journals plus letters and assorted documents, there are mostly just hints about what firearms the various individuals carried. The following list is a well-reasoned, educated guess of who carried what firearm. The list assumes all accouterments that go with a weapon. It also assumes that either personal knives and tomahawks or ones from Harper's Ferry were available to all. "Unknown" means there is no information on what, if any, weapons the person had when joining the expedition.

Who Carried What

	Before Joining Expedition	Members of Permanent Party (*)	Probable Weapons
Lewis, Meriwether	Secretary to President Jefferson	*	Personal rifle, air rifle, fowling piece, 2 pistols, sword, espontoon
Clark, William	Retired artillery captain	*	Personal rifle, 2 pistols, sword, maybe espontoon, maybe fusil
Floyd, Charles (sergeant)	1 of 9 young men from Kentucky		Personal rifle
Gass, Patrick (sergeant)	Capt. Russell Bissell's 1st Infantry Co.	*	Model 1795 musket
Ordway, John (sergeant)	Capt. Russell Bissell's 1st Infantry Co.	*	Model 1795 musket
Pryor, Nathaniel (sergeant)	1 of 9 young men from Kentucky	*	Personal rifle
Warfington, Richard (corporal)	Capt. John Campbell's 2nd Infantry Co.		Model 1795 musket
Boley, John	Capt. Russell Bissell's 1st Infantry Co.		Model 1795 musket
Bratton, William E.	1 of 9 young men from Kentucky	*	Personal rifle
Collins, John	Capt. Russell Bissell's 1st Infantry Co.	*	Model 1795 musket
Charbonneau, Toussaint (interpreter)	Trader in the Mandan Villages	*	Personal rifle
Charbonneau, Sacagawea	Wife of Toussaint C.	*	No firearm

Charbonneau, J. Baptiste	Born January, 1805		No firearm
Colter, John	1 of 9 young men from Kentucky	*	Personal rifle
Cruzatte, Pierre	Missouri River boatman	*	Unknown
Dame, John	Capt. Amos Stoddard's Artillery Co.		Model 1795 musket
Drouillard, George (interpreter)	Possibly worked as an interpreter for U.S. Army	*	Personal rifle
Field, Joseph	1 of 9 young men from Kentucky	*	Personal rifle
Field, Reuben	1 of 9 young men from Kentucky	*	Personal rifle
Frazer, Robert	Unknown	*	Personal rifle
Gibson, George	1 of 9 young men from Kentucky		Personal rifle
Goodrich, Silas	Unknown	*	Unknown
Hall, Hugh	Capt. John Campbell's 2nd Infantry Co.	*	Model 1795 musket
Howard, Thomas P.	Capt. John Campbell's 2nd Infantry Co.	*	Model 1795 musket
Labiche, Francois	Boatman and interpreter	*	Unknown
Lepage, Jean Baptiste	Living at Mandan Villages	*	Unknown
McNeal, Hugh	Unknown		Unknown
Newman, John	Capt. Daniel Bissell's 1st Infantry Co.		Model 1795 musket
Potts, John	Capt. Robert Purdy's Co.	*	Model 1795 musket

	Before Joining Expedition	Members of Permanent Party (*)	Probable Weapons
Reed, Moses B.	Unknown		Unknown (perhaps not well armed; he took a short rifle when he deserted)
Robertson, John	Capt. Amos Stoddard's Artillery Co.		Model 1795 musket
Shannon, George	1 of 9 young men from Kentucky	*	Personal rifle
Shields, John	1 of 9 young men from Kentucky	*	Personal rifle
Thompson, John B.	Unknown	*	Unknown
Tuttle, Ebenezer	Capt. Amos Stoddard's Artillery Co.		Model 1795 musket
Weiser, Peter M.	Capt. Russell Bissell's 1st Infantry Co.	*	Model 1795 musket
Werner, William	Unknown	*	Unknown
White, Issac	Capt. Amos Stoddard's Artillery Co.		Model 1795 musket
Whitehouse, Joseph	Capt. Daniel Bissell's 1st Infantry Co.	*	Model 1795 musket
Willard, Alexander Hamilton	Capt. Amos Stoddard's Artillery Co.	*	Model 1795 musket
Windsor, Richard	Capt. Russell Bissell's 1st Infantry Co.	*	Model 1795 musket
York	William Clark's slave	*	Personal rifle

Engagés	Professional boatmen	Unknown
Conn, E.		
Congee, Charles		
Collins, Joseph		
Deschamps, Jean Baptiste (patron–foreman)		
Hebert, Charles		
La Jennesse, Jean Baptiste		
La Liberte		
Malbeouf, Etienne		
Pinant, Peter		
Primeau, Paul		
Rivet, Francois		
Roi, Peter		

The Care and Feeding
of the Flintlock

In the fall of 2001, as the war in Afghanistan loomed, the *Washington Post* ran an article on today's military rifles. Everyone I questioned about the arms they saw in the media (and these were decidedly not gun folks) already knew that all these weapons had high-capacity magazines. Newspapers, movies, television, and the web have given most people in this country enough knowledge at least to understand that many of today's weapons are capable of firing a lot of bullets in a hurry. These same people, confronted with an early nineteenth century flintlock Kentucky rifle, would see the beauty of the elegant lines and craftsmanship of the weapon, but might have trouble imagining that it was once the cutting edge of technology. They would have even more trouble figuring out how it worked. Some understanding of the history of firearms will help here.

The earliest guns were cannons, built by bell makers, who alone possessed the technical skills to forge something that large and strong. These firearms were loaded by pouring gun powder down the barrel's *bore*, the inside of the barrel, and shoving a stone of roughly the same size as the bore down on top of the powder. At the back of the bore a small pinhole, the *touch hole*, was drilled from the top of the barrel through the weapon to the bore. Once the gun was loaded and aimed, more gunpowder was poured down the touch hole, with a bit left on top of the barrel. To fire the gun, a *slow match* (a smoldering cord designed for the purpose) was touched to the pile of powder at the touch hole. Once ignited, the powder burned through the hole into the bore and set off the powder there, which, exploding, sent the stone sailing off in ways not predicted by Aristotle. Luckily for the development of firearms, the artillerists ignored the theological and philosophical implications of the arched flight path of the stones and went about the practical geometry of knocking down castle walls from a distance.

Given the human propensity to fiddle with new technologies, various weapon makers soon began to experiment with hand cannons, weapons small enough for a man to hold and fire by hand. Of course, to hold the hand cannon steady enough to keep the little pile of gunpowder on top of the barrel from shaking off, and to both aim and touch the powder with the hand-held slow match required an absolute minimum of two hands, and three would have been better. Various makers began tinkering with a mechanism for holding the slow match and moving it mechanically to the powder, and with ways of keeping the powder from shaking off the top of the barrel.

The result of the first was the creation of the *serpentine*, a curved piece designed to hold the slow match above the barrel and extend below the barrel as well; the shooter could grasp that extension with the forefinger of the hand he was using to steady the weapon against his shoulder. A pivot pin at the device's midpoint allowed the shooter to fire the weapon simply by pulling back on the lower extension, a movement that pushed the upper end of the serpentine, with the slow match in its jaws, down into the powder.

To solve the second problem, the *pan* was invented. It was quite literally a pan, a depression to hold the powder so that shaking or slight tipping wouldn't dump it off the barrel. Piling all these additions to the top of the barrel made aiming more than a little difficult, so the result was to place the pan on the side of the barrel. This weapon—heavy, tough, and inaccurate, but far better than the older hand cannon—was called the *matchlock*.

There were other improvements. The *lock*, the mechanism joining the trigger and serpentine, became a relatively standardized, mechanically durable type. The bullet was no longer the round, smooth river rock of the original cannons. Lead had become the standard material for making spherical bullets, *balls* for the shoulder and hand-fired weapons. The ball continued in use until the middle of the nineteenth century.

The next major innovation involved moving away from the slow-match ignition system to one based on the mineral- and steel-produced spark. Everywhere guns were made, flint and steel had been used as a fire starter for many centuries. Striking flint to steel threw sparks that could be caught in a tinder material, which could then be nursed into a fire. By throwing a spark into a gun's pan, the gunpowder could be ignited without the necessity of carrying and nursing a slow match while waiting to shoot. One of the first successful systems for spark ignition was the *wheel lock*, which did not use flint but pyrite. The weapon's firing mechanism used a rough-edged steel wheel larger than but similar to the ones on today's cigarette lighters. The wheel was moved by a coiled spring that had to be wound. The serpentine's mouth had been modified from a tube to hold the slow match to a vise that tightly gripped a piece of iron pyrite. To fire it, one loaded the weapon and wound its wheel spring, moving the serpentine so that the pyrite was in contact with the wheel's rough edge directly above the pan. When the trigger was pulled, the coiled spring attached to the wheel was released, spinning it against the pyrite and throwing sparks from it into the powder-filled pan. Fire from that explosion passed through the touch hole and set off the powder in the gun's chamber, sending the ball down the barrel.

The wheel lock was a much more certain ignition system than the matchlock. But it was delicate, wonderful as a sporting arm but not rugged enough for military use, so the tinkering continued.

There was an intermediate step between the wheel lock and the flintlock. It was called the *snaphance*. The idea behind it was essentially the same as the flintlock, and it can be thought of as the first weapon actually to use a flint-and steel-ignition system. The hammer or *cock*, as the serpentine was then called, held a piece of flint instead of the iron pyrite of the wheel lock. But now the hammer was propelled against a steel striking plate by a spring. Flint struck steel, and the resulting sparks landed in the powder-filled pan, beginning the firing chain. However, like the wheel lock, the snaphance was too delicate for military use. The snaphance soon evolved into the *flintlock*, a reliable and rugged weapon that was the standard weapon for military and sporting use. Taking the combined life spans of the snaphance and the flintlock, striking flint to steel was the firing mechanism for firearms for two and half centuries.

A gun's lock is the mechanism that fires the weapon. The lock of the flintlock was mounted on the side of the weapon, at the rear of the barrel. The size of the lock obviously varied depending on the size of the weapon, but on the average rifle or musket of the late eighteenth or early nineteenth centuries the lock would have been about four inches or so long. It consisted of a lock plate to which most of the moving parts were attached. On the outside of the lock (exposed on the outside of the gun) was the cock, or *hammer*, which held the flint in a screw-tightened jaw; the pan, attached to a reinforcing bolster to give it sufficient mass; the *frizzen*, an L-shaped piece of iron or steel that functioned both as a protective cover for the pan and as the steel striking plate for the flint. The frizzen is held in place by a V-shaped spring. This spring held the frizzen in place, keeping the pan covered and the powder in it until the gun was fired. It gave the frizzen sufficient resistance to the striking flint to make sure sparks were thrown, but not too much so that it would flip up and expose the pan to the sparks of the impact.

On the inside of the lock plate are the *mainspring*, the *tumbler*, the *bridle*, and the *sear*, held under tension by its own spring. The arrangement allowed the cock to be placed in three positions. *Full cock* is the position of maximum tension on the mainspring.

The tumbler and bridle holds all this tension because the sear holds everything in place under the tension of the mainspring. When the trigger is pulled, it pushes the sear loose from its contact with the tumbler, allowing the mainspring to move the cock rapidly and strongly against the frizzen and causing the gun to fire. Between these two positions is the *half cock*, or safety position. Here the trigger cannot be pulled, and the cock is not in contact with the frizzen. That means the weapon can be loaded and the pan charged and then safely covered with the frizzen. Then all that is required to fire is to go to full cock, aim, and pull the trigger. There is always the risk of the safety not working—hence the phrase "going off half-cocked." The trigger assembly is actually a fairly simple mechanism; it allows the person to use only a slight amount of finger pressure to release all the stored energy of the springs, which then move the cock with enough energy to cause the system to work.

For the firing chain to continue past the pan—to not have just a flash in the pan—it was necessary for the barrel to have a touch hole, which worked the same way that all guns had since the first cannons. What happened once the pan's fire ignited the powder in the gun's barrel depended on a number of things at that time. Assuming the weapon was well made and clean, the leading factor in what happened was whether the gun's bore was *smooth* or *rifled*. A smooth-bored gun, as the name implies, was smooth along the inside of the barrel, which presented some problems for the flintlock. The gunpowder of the late eighteenth and early nineteenth centuries was not clean burning, which resulted in fouling of the barrel: powder residue collected along the bore, particularly the front end. For a military musket, that translated into a serious problem, since over the course of a battle, enough residues could build up to effectively reduce the diameter of the bore. The result was that the U.S. Army's Model 1795 musket with a .69-caliber bore fired a .63-caliber ball—which resulted in the ball, in effect, rattling down the barrel. This made aiming a less-than-certain art, since the direction of the ball's flight would be along the vector determined by the last impact with the barrel, which was not necessarily the direction in which the gun was being aimed. To try to help resolve this problem, the militaries throughout the world issued paper cartridges, each of which contained gunpowder and a ball.

Before a Model 1795 musket was loaded, it was checked to make sure the flint and frizzen were dry and the bore was free of moisture or oil (used to protect the metal during storage). To load the musket a soldier, who needed to be standing erect, held the gun at its balance point with his left hand. Putting the hammer at half cock, the soldier then flipped the frizzen forward and used the *vent pick*, a wire of the proper stiffness and diameter, to clean any fouling from the touch hole and a stiff-bristled brush to clean the pan. He then removed a paper cartridge from the cartouche box he carried, usually at waist level but held on a shoulder strap. He bit the end off the cartridge and dumped a small amount of gunpowder into the pan, which he then sealed in by closing the frizzen over it. Then, with the butt of the gun on the ground so that the weapon was slightly tilted (this was important, since the Model 1795 was about five feet long and the man who was loading it was likely not much taller) and holding the gun near the muzzle with his left hand, the soldier used his right hand to dump the rest of the powder down the barrel. Next he used all, part, or none of the paper from the cartridge—depending on how much burnt powder residue was in the barrel—to get the ball to seat properly in the barrel and started the ball down the barrel with his thumb. Then he extracted the ramrod from its holding tube, which ran the full length of the barrel through the stock's forearm, and used it to push the ball, powder, and any of the paper wadding down the length of the bore and seat it firmly at the breech end of the barrel, where the touch hole entered the chamber. Withdrawing the ramrod from the barrel, the soldier returned it to its holding pipe and then brought the musket across his chest, changing the grip of his left hand back to the balance point. Bringing the musket to his shoulder, he used his right hand to bring the hammer to full cock, aimed, and squeezed the trigger.

If his aim was true and if he didn't flinch from either the anticipation of the recoil or from the flash of the powder exploding in the pan, and if he had properly wadded the ball with the paper cartridge so the ball didn't ricochet off the end of the barrel, the ball sailed down range and hit what was intended. In other words the musket was an inherently inaccurate weapon. It was designed to be used at close range and in volley fire at a massed target, such as opposing ranks of soldiers. At close range, fifty yards or less, the huge lead ball, just under an ounce in weight, was devastating.

It was also easy to load a musket with shot. Birdshot, pellets the size of modern-day BBs or smaller, is designed for hunting birds and small game. Buckshot, much larger pellets (but still considerably smaller than the gun's bore diameter), is designed for use against larger animals, such as buck deer, or humans. The theory behind the use of shot is that it is easier to hit something with a handful of pebbles than with a single rock. Its main disadvantages are that the range of shot is considerably less than that of a single projectile of roughly the same caliber and that shot loses power much more quickly. Buckshot was considered excellent for defensive uses by most armies at the time of the expedition. In fact, as they prepared to leave Camp Dubois, on May 10, 1804, William Clark wrote, "order every man to have 100 Balls for ther Rifles & 2 lb. Of Buck Shot for those with mussquets."[1]

Muskets were made for ease of loading. The flintlock rifle, such as the ones some of the men would have brought with them and the ones Lewis had brought from Harper's Ferry, were considerably different from the Model 1795 muskets. While the firing system is the same, the bore of the rifle is radically different. That difference is the *rifling*, grooves that spiral the length of the bore. The exact origin of rifling is unknown, but the best guess

---

[1]Moulton, *Journals of the Lewis and Clark Expedition*, 2:213.

puts it somewhere in Central Europe in the late fifteenth or early sixteenth centuries. It's one of those ideas that may not have had a single point of origin, because it combined in one element the solution to two problems. The first problem: gunpowder burned dirty. Grooving the bore of a gun allowed for reduced friction between ball and barrel, since fouling tended to accumulate in the grooves, rather than on the raised portion of the bore. The second problem? Accuracy, and the solution, well understood as early as the fifteenth century, was that rotation stabilizes a moving sphere. If the grooves were spiraled down the bore, they caused the ball to spin, greatly improving the weapon's accuracy.

Why were muskets still in use two hundred years after the invention of rifling? Loading is the answer. A well-trained soldier could fire about four rounds from a musket in the same amount of time that it took a well-trained rifleman to fire one, and on the open, close-range battlefields of the day, that was significant.

As with the musket, the length of the rifles at the beginning of the nineteenth century, four to five feet, suggests that they were most easily loaded while the rifleman was standing. Riflemen as a rule carried loose powder in a horn or flask, rather than premeasured paper cartridges. Powder had to be measured either with a spring-closed tube attached to the flask or by using a measuring cup that held the right amount of powder. Powder was poured from the horn into the cup, then from the cup into the rifle barrel. Since the ball was slightly smaller than the bore, a patch was required to seal the bullet to the bore, sizing it to the bore to give a good, tight fit and marry the ball to the rifling grooves. The patch also made sure that the ball, once pressed against the powder at the breech, stayed put, preventing any separation between the exploding gunpowder and the ball. A gap between the two could cause excessive pressure to build up in the space that could weaken the barrel and could result in the barrel exploding.

Lubricating the patch made it easier to force the ball down the barrel and helped with the seal between the two. There were two general forms of lubricant: grease (such as tallow) or saliva.

(*left*) View inside a rifle barrel, showing the spiral grooves of the rifling that impart spin to the ball or bullet. (*right*) View of bore of rifle showing the grooves of the rifling. The bumps on the circular bore that give it an angular appearance are the ends of the rifling grooves. *Both photos courtesy Michael F. Carrick.*

Many Kentucky rifles had patch boxes built into the right side of the stock, just in front of the butt plate. Greased patches could be kept there. Of course, many riflemen kept other things there and put their patches in their "possible sacks," the pouches with all their needed accouterments. Patches might be cut to size or in long strips of the right width. The rifleman might hold the strip in his mouth to keep it lubricated with saliva, then place one end of the strip over the muzzle and start a ball down the muzzle. Using a small knife carried on the strap of his possible sack, he then cut the appropriate amount off the strip and returned the remainder to his mouth. If he carried lubricated strips, the process was the same except that the strip would be in his possible sack rather than in his mouth. If he had precut patches, then the process would be the same, save the cutting. The lubrication, oil or saliva, did not have a serious effect on the powder with which it was in contact. Patches could, in a pinch, be made of any cloth or soft leather. But to work properly it was important to use the right material: cloth that was uniform, tightly woven

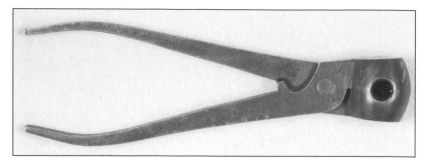

BULLET MOLD

A mold such as this one, designed to make one ball at a time, was easy
for an individual to carry and would have been kept in the bag with
other tools necessary for the care and feeding of the man's weapons.
Courtesy Michael F. Carrick.

and durable, such as mattress ticking or linen. Once beyond the
reaches of civilization, probably the best field expedient in the
American West was pronghorn hides. Buckskin from a young
deer would work almost as well.

At the beginning of the nineteenth century, balls fired by rifles
were most likely made by the rifleman who shot them. The balls
were made by melting lead in a heavy, long-handled ladle over
a fire. The melted lead was poured into a bullet mold the rifleman carried with him. Meriwether Lewis had designed gunpowder canisters made of lead. Each of the canisters weighed about
eight pounds and held about four pounds of powder. When more
ammunition was needed, a canister was emptied of its powder,
which was transferred to powder horns, and the canister itself was
cut into pieces and then melted down as a joint venture by several
men, each of whom possessed a bullet mold that shaped a ball
of the caliber matching their rifles. Most riflemen would have a
one- or two-ball mold, but there were, especially for the muskets,
gang molds that could make one to two dozen balls at once.

When making balls, care was needed; imperfect balls made
for inaccurate shots. And there were imperfections built into the

GANG MOLD

A bullet mold such as this one could make a number of balls at once by pouring molten lead into each hole in turn. These were designed in a variety of ball sizes, from large musket balls to small birdshot. *Courtesy Michael F. Carrick.*

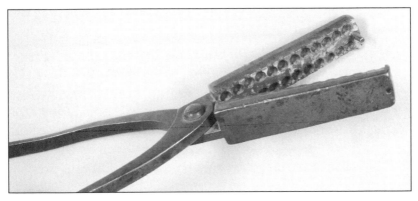

GANG MOLD

This view shows the mold opened, revealing the multiple balls this one made in one pouring—twenty-four. This one is for shot rather than musket or rifle balls. *Courtesy Michael F. Carrick.*

process. The mold design left a slight nipple on the ball that had to be trimmed off with a knife. If there was time when loading, that rough spot would be placed so it was at the back of the bore, against the powder charge, not along the side, so it would be along the axis of rotation and wouldn't affect the bullet's spin.

Lead was the preferred metal for balls for several reasons, including cost, weight, sectional density, and low melting temperature. Many metals were tried—iron, brass, tin, bronze, even gold and silver—but all were rejected, since lead worked best. For folks on the frontier the low melting point was important, and a campfire produced more than enough heat to melt lead.

Proper *flints* were essential for the flintlock. Since flint knapping was a technology that had been around for tens of thousands of years, one might assume that everyone made his own gun flints, but such was generally not the case. The vast majority of gun flints used in America at the time of the expedition were manufactured in either France or England, and each flint was hand crafted. A good craftsman could knock off about a thousand chips a day, from which he could produce about five hundred finished flints. According to the U.S. Army of the mid-nineteenth century, the gun flint had an ". . . edge or bevel, the back, the sides, the face, slightly convex, and the bed, or lower face, slightly concave . . . a good flint will last for more than fifty fires. . . ."[2] Even with that assurance the army issued one flint for every twenty rounds of ammunition. Of course beyond the reach of European trade, Lewis and Clark or anyone else of the period had access to skilled flint knappers. Certainly there were knappers in every tribe who could produce gun flints as needed, though trade records show that the tribes largely traded for the flints along with the ammunition.

The patched ball was best started down a rifle barrel with a *ball starter*, a one- to three-inch ramrod with a two- to three-inch diameter wooden ball palm rest at the top. This allowed the rifleman to exert maximum pressure on the patched ball and set it properly into the grooves. Once the ball starter was returned to his "possible sack," the rifleman withdrew his ramrod from below the rifle's barrel and forced the powder and patched ball down the barrel to the breech—and "forced" is the operative word. Pushing the patched ball down the grooved bore of the rifle takes time and energy, which is the reason armies of that day still preferred muskets. With conscript or minimally trained

---

[2] *Ordnance Manual of the United States Army*, 1850 edition. Quoted in Harold Peterson's *Encyclopedia of Firearms*, 146.

volunteers, four shots to one was preferred, especially when you didn't trust the accuracy of either the four or the one shot. Riflemen needed training.

Once the ball was seated against the powder in the breech, the ramrod was drawn from the bore and returned to its holder under the barrel. The pan was then charged with, usually, a finer grained powder than that used in the barrel, to give a better burn and a surer continuation of the firing train. This powder was carried in a small horn or flask, and though many of the flasks had a measuring system similar to that of the larger flasks that carried barrel powder, it was one measurement that was easy to estimate.

The Corps of Discovery's pistols and blunderbusses would have been loaded and fired the same way as their muskets. The swivel was a small piece of artillery, and though loaded as a musket, would have been fired in a manner more like the hand cannon described above.

The "possible sack" in which a rifleman carried all his shooting accouterments was generally a haversack from six inches to a foot and a half long, about as wide as long and two to four inches deep. Ideally, the cleaning pin and brush for the touch hole and the pan would be easily accessible, perhaps on a cord attached to the shoulder strap. A small knife, for such things as trimming patches, might also be carried in a small sheath either on the outside of the sack or on the shoulder strap. Inside the sack a rifleman carried balls, patches, spare flints, cleaning equipment, a ball screw, a worm, and probably a few odds and ends that the individual considered important for shooting well or being comfortable while in the field. William Clark, for example, carried a short length of slow match in his. Perhaps it was to help start fires, though the only time he recorded using it was as part of a magic show to impress some Indians.

Along with the possible sack, the rifleman would carry one or two powder horns or flasks. The larger one carried the powder for the rifle, the smaller one carried the finer grained powder for the pan. The larger one was carried over the shoulder in the same manner as the possible sack, while the smaller might be carried on the same strap, on its own strap, or inside the possible sack. If the larger horn or flask didn't have a spring-loaded measure built into it, the cup sized for the right amount of powder might be attached to the shoulder strap, or carried inside the possible sack.

Comparing the Corps of Discovery's flintlocks to today's military assault rifles, Squad Automatic Weapons (sAWs), and sniper rifles may make the Corps seem poorly armed. But they felt, with reason, that they were the best armed group ever to head up the Missouri. They were well pleased with their modern firearms, as are the soldiers of today's army. Times change, but soldiers who are satisfied that they are well armed perform better, today or two hundred years ago.

Glossary

AIR GUN   Any gun that uses compressed air as its source of power.

AMMUNITION   All the expendable materials used for each firing of a weapon. For a flintlock it includes the ball, the gunpowder, the patch or paper cartridge, and a bit of the flint.

ARMORY   Technically a place to manufacture arms, but often used to denote an arms storage facility. Today it also describes a facility for military reserve or national guard units.

ARSENAL   A place for the storage of arms, but in this country also used for arms manufacturing complexes. In this country, "arsenal" and "armory" are often used interchangeably.

BALL   The spherical bullet of the flintlock. Balls are of a slightly smaller diameter than the bore diameter of the weapon.

BALLISTICS   The study of the motion of projectiles. For shooters, figuring out how to hit what is being aimed at.

BALL SCREW   A screw device that can be attached to the end of a ramrod and used to extract a ball from a muzzle loader without firing the weapon.

BANDS   The metal straps that attach the forearm of a rifle or musket to the barrel.

BARREL   The tube through which a gun's bullet is fired toward its target.

BATTERY   *See* frizzen.

BAYONET   A pointed and sometimes edged weapon attached to the end of a rifle or musket to convert it into a thrusting spear for close combat. These replaced the pike and were important for armies until the advent of rapid-fire, quick reloading rifles.

BLACK POWDER   A term used to differentiate the older, dark-colored mixture of saltpeter, charcoal, and sulfur from the modern gun powders such as cordite.

BLUNDERBUSS   A large, smooth-bored weapon whose bore expands into a wide flared bell at the muzzle. It is generally thought that the name is derived from the German *Dunder* (thunder) and *Buchse* (gun).

BORE   The inside of a gun's barrel.

BORE BRUSH   A brush, usually of a metal such as copper, used to clean the bore of a weapon.

BREECH   The back of a gun's barrel.

BULL BOAT   A round boat made by stretching a green buffalo hide over a willow frame. Used by Plains Indians, usually for crossing rivers.

BULLET   The projectile of a firearm or air gun. During the flintlock era, bullets were balls. Since the middle of the nineteenth century, modified cones have been the preferred shape.

BULLET MOLD   A mold into which melted lead can be poured to form bullets. During the time of the expedition, these could be single-ball molds or gang molds, which might shape as many as twenty or more balls at a time.

BUTT   The end of the gun stock closest to the shooter. For a musket or rifle it is the part of the stock that fits against the shooter's shoulder. For a pistol it is the bottom of the grip.

BUTT PLATE   A metal fitting around a gun butt to reinforce and protect it.

CALIBER   A measure of the diameter of a bullet or the bore of a rifle. Caliber is measured as decimal for inches; e.g., .50 caliber is .50 inch.

CANOE   A light, narrow boat propelled by paddles. Throughout the areas the Corps of Discovery traveled, canoes were dugouts, made by hollowing out logs.

CARBINE   A short shoulder arm. At the time of the expedition, members of the Corps of Discovery were more likely to use the term "fusil" or "fusee."

CARTOUCHE   A French word for a paper cartridge. The Lewis and Clark journalists used the term only in reference to cartridge boxes. The cartouche boxes were leather boxes carried on the belt or a shoulder strap. There was a wooden block inside that had holes bored in it to accommodate paper cartridges.

CARTRIDGE   The container for one shot's powder and bullet. Today's cartridges are metal or waterproof plastic cases with the primer mounted in the base and powder inside. The bullet or shot are either attached to the front or inside. In the Corps's time, it was the powder and ball, or shot, for a musket rolled into a paper tube whose ends were either folded or twisted together.

CHAMBER   The back of the gun's bore where the powder and lead are placed prior to firing.

COCK   On a flintlock, the piece of the firing mechanism that held the flint. Also called *hammer*. During the flintlock period there were two basic cock designs, the elegant but more delicate gooseneck, an S-shaped piece reminiscent of the matchlock's serpentine, and the more rugged double neck, in which the vise screw protruded into the space between the two necks.

DIRK   A double edged fixed blade knife with a sharp point.

DRAM   Technically ⅛ ounce, but often used to mean a small drink.

ESPONTOON (OR SPONTOON)   A half pike. The pike was a type of spear, sixteen to eighteen feet in length, designed to protect musketeers from cavalry during the lengthy reloading process. It was replaced by the bayonet. The espontoon was a short version, roughly six feet long, used as a walking stick or spear. The espontoon was carried by infantry lieutenants and captains as a badge of rank that men could see on the march and the battlefield.

EYEDAG   A dagger with a hole in the handle for inserting a cord or loop. These were popular with tribes of the Pacific Northwest coast who did not want to risk losing a knife out of a boat.

FIREARM   Any weapon that shoots a projectile by the use of a gunpowder explosion.

FIRELOCK   The U.S. Army's term for its flintlocks. In colonial times the name was in common use to describe any firearm. By the beginning of the nineteenth century, only the army was still using the term.

FLASH HOLE   The vent from the breech of any muzzle-loading gun that allows the priming flash to reach the powder in the chamber.

FLINT   A hard, silica-rich stone similar to chalcedony used as a worked stone and a fire-starting agent for thousands of years. For the flintlock the term is used to describe a manufactured wedge of flint held in the cock's vise that throws sparks when it strikes the frizzen, igniting the powder in the pan and firing the weapon.

FLINTLOCK   A firearm utilizing flint and steel to strike sparks to ignite the priming powder.

FOREARM   The part of a gun's stock that extends under the barrel.

FORGE   A blacksmith's hearth with a system, such as a bellows, that allows the smith to heat metals to high enough temperatures for shaping and tempering.

FOWLING PIECE   A smooth bored gun designed to fire shot and used for bird and small game hunting. A shotgun.

FRIZZEN   The part of the flintlock's lock that the flint strikes to produce sparks. It is sometimes called *steel* or *battery*.

FUSE   Any cord containing or saturated with combustible materials that assures a steady burn. Fuses are used to set off explosives, or during the time of the expedition, to fire cannons.

FUSEE (FUZEE)   The English form of the French *fusil*. To the French, *fusée* meant a rocket.

FUSIL   A French short-barreled, lightweight musket used instead of a standard musket by special troops and cavalry. In this country the term, or *fusee*, was used to describe any short, shoulder-fired weapon, much as the term *carbine* is used today.

GAUGE   The measure of a gun's bore diameter using the number of lead balls of that diameter needed to weigh one pound. For instance, a gun requiring twelve balls to weigh one pound would be called a *12 gauge*. Today the system is used for smooth-bored weapons such as shotguns.

GRAIN   The unit used to measure gunpowder, ⅟₅₄ of an ounce or .0648 grams.

GROOVES   The spiral channels cut into the bore of a rifle barrel to impart spin to the bullet, improving its accuracy.

GUN LOCK   The mechanism for firing a gun. On a flintlock the lock included the cock (hammer), the frizzen, the pan, and a set of sears and springs that allowed the trigger to drop the cock with sufficient power to throw sparks into the pan when it strikes the frizzen, firing the weapon.

GUNPOWDER   The explosive mixture of potassium nitrate, sulfur, and charcoal used to fire guns. During the flintlock period, it took roughly one-half pound of powder to shoot one pound of lead.

GUNSMITH   Someone who builds and/or repairs guns. At the beginning of the nineteenth century many frontier blacksmiths were also gunsmiths.

GUNSTOCK   The part of a gun on which the barrel and lock are mounted (as in "lock, stock, and barrel"). Until the mid- to late twentieth century, gunstocks were normally made of wood.

HALF COCK   On a hammered weapon, a safety position where the hammer cannot be tripped by the trigger. On a flintlock, the hammer, or cock, is midway between the frizzen and the full cocked position. The half cock as a safety position is not infallible, hence the term "going off half-cocked," meaning doing something before one is aimed and ready.

HAMMER   The part of a firearm that strikes the frizzen, cap, or primer and fires the weapon. On a flintlock *hammer* and *cock* are two names for the same part.

JAWS   On a flintlock cock, the vise that holds the flint.

KEELBOAT   Literally, a boat with a keel. On American rivers in the eighteenth and nineteenth centuries a keelboat was a river cargo vessel designed to work with sail, oars, punt poles, or tow line. The Corps's boat, designed by Lewis, did not resemble the typical American keelboat but looked more like a Spanish river galley.

KENTUCKY RIFLE   A long-barreled, elegant rifle, often of relatively small caliber, popular along the trans-Appalachian frontier. The name derives from the popular concept of Kentucky as the frontier exemplar. It was also called the "Pennsylvania rifle," because the design was developed and perfected in that state.

LANDS   The part of the rifle bore between the grooves. This is the bore diameter before cutting the rifling into the barrel.

LOCK   Same as gun lock.

LOCK PLATE   The metal plate to which the parts of the lock are affixed. On a flintlock, the plate is normally on the right side of the weapon and holds, on the outside, the cock, frizzen, pan, and the frizzen spring. On the inside it holds all the necessary pins, springs, and sears.

LONG RIFLE   Same as Kentucky rifle.

MAINSPRING   The spring that powers the fall of the hammer.

MUSKET   Originally, a term applied to heavy, large-bored, shoulder-fired weapons that required a rest to fire. By the nineteenth century the term was applied to the standard smooth-bored weapons of the infantry, such as the U.S. Army's Model 1795.

MATCHLOCK   An early firearm in which the powder in the pan was ignited by a slow-burning cord, the match.

MUZZLE   The front of a gun barrel.

MUZZLE LOADER   Any gun that is loaded by ramming the powder and bullet down the barrel from the front end.

PAN   The receptacle for the priming powder on the flintlock and its forebears. On the flintlock the pan is covered by the frizzen until the cock falls.

PAN BRUSH   A stiff-bristled brush used to clean the powder residue from the pan.

PATCH   A piece of fabric, leather, or paper used to create a snug fit for a ball in a muzzle-loading weapon. Patches were considered vital to the accuracy of rifles during the flintlock period.

PATCH BOX   A box cut into the right side of the stock, at the butt, of a Kentucky rifle, designed to hold spare patches.

PENNSYLVANIA RIFLE   Same as the Kentucky rifle. The two names can be used interchangeably, though the Kentucky name is more commonly heard.

PIROGUE   Normally a dugout boat, but Lewis and Clark used the term to apply to boats larger than canoes but smaller than keelboats.

PISTOL   Any short firearm intended to be fired with one hand. A horseman's pistol of the early nineteenth century was large and large bored. It was intended to be carried in a holster attached to the saddle, so it normally came in pairs to balance the weight. Pocket pistols were smaller, usually of a relatively small caliber. They were meant to be carried on the person but in the pocket rather than a holster. In the eighteenth and nineteenth centuries, there were coats designed with pockets to hold pistols.

PORTFIRE   A slow-burning fuse. Though portfires and slow matches had different chemicals in them, Lewis and Clark used the names interchangeably.

POWDER   Here the same as gunpowder.

POWDER HORN   A container made of horn (bull horn was preferred for size and durability) for holding gunpowder. The base end was plugged, normally with wood, and the tip was drilled out and stoppered so that, with the stopper removed, powder could be poured out.

POWDER MEASURE   A device for measuring the amount of powder needed for each shot of a muzzle loader.

PRIMING   In a flintlock, the powder put into the pan to begin the firing process. It was often of finer grains than the powder used in the bore.

PRIMING HORN   A powder horn used to hold the priming powder.

RAM PIPES   Ferrules used to hold the ramrod under the barrel of a muzzle loader.

RAMROD   A rod of wood or metal used to force the powder and bullet of a muzzle loader to the chamber at the back of the bore. It is carried in the ram pipes.

RECOIL   The force pushing a firearm backward as a reaction to the expulsion of the projectile, according to Newton's third law of motion.

RIFLE   A shoulder-fired gun with spiraling grooves cut into the bore to impart a stabilizing spin to the bullet.

RIFLING   The grooves in the bore of a rifle.

SAFETY   Any mechanism for locking the firing mechanism of a gun. (*See* half cock.)

SALUTE GUN   Any small cannon used as a means of signaling.

SCIMITAR   Technically, a curve-bladed, single-edged sword of the Middle East. Lewis and Clark used the term to denote a double-edged, straight-bladed weapon they saw around the mouth of the Columbia.

SEAR   The part of a gun's lock that holds the mainspring in tension when the weapon is cocked. The trigger trips the sear, releasing the mainspring to drive the hammer forward.

SERPENTINE   The S-curved cock of a matchlock. It held the slow match and lowered it into the priming charge when the weapon was fired.

SET TRIGGER   A second trigger on a gun that sets the other trigger, allowing a very light pressure on it to fire the weapon.

SHOT   Pellets much smaller than the gun's bore diameter, allowing many to be fired at once. It came in two forms: buckshot, larger-size shot designed for large game, such as buck deer, or humans; and birdshot, smaller shot designed for birds or small game.

SIDEARM   Any weapon intended to be carried on the person and generally to be used with one hand. Though normally thought of as pistols, knives, swords, and tomahawks would all qualify as sidearms.

SIGHTS   The device along a gun's barrel designed to aid in aiming. At the time of the expedition, rifles generally had a front sight that was a post or blade and a rear sight that was a notch through which the front sight could be centered and placed on line with the target. Muskets often had only the front sight.

SLING   A strap of leather or fabric attached to a gun to allow it to be carried more easily and comfortably and/or to aid in steadying the weapon while aiming.

SMALL ARMS   Guns that can be carried by an individual and fired without support.

SMOOTHBORE   Any gun without rifling.

SLOW MATCH   A slow-burning fuse similar to a portfire; a punk.

SNAPHANCE   A forerunner of the true flintlock in which the frizzen was not the pan cover. The snaphance was generally considered too delicate and complicated for use as a military weapon.

STOCK   Same as gunstock.

SWIVEL GUN   A small cannon meant to be mounted on a wall or vessel and used as a weapon, for salutes, or for both.

SWIVELS   Hinged metal loops attached to the gunstock and/or trigger guard that allows the sling to be attached to the gun.

SWORD   An edged weapon with a long blade and designed to be used with one or both hands. Swords have also been a badge of rank for many centuries.

TOMAHAWK   A lightweight, one-handed ax used as a tool and weapon. The term was originally Algonquian and referred to a specific type of stone-headed war club. The colonists borrowed the word, which came to refer to a variety of styles of light axes but all close enough in design to be recognized as the same thing. The pipe tomahawk had an ax blade on one side of the head and a pipe bowl on the other. The handle had a channel bored in it to connect to the pipe bowl.

TOUCH HOLE   Same as flash hole.

TRADE GUN   Any gun designed for trading purposes. In North America the trade guns were designed for the Indian trade. While the weapons were never of the highest quality, they did have to be of high enough grade not to wear out too quickly or the Indians would have stopped trading for them, or perhaps stopped trading at all. During the flintlock period, trade guns were usually smooth bored.

TRAJECTORY   The path of a projectile's flight.

TRIGGER   The device, usually a lever projecting from the bottom of the weapon, beneath the lock, used to release the sear and begin the firing process.

TRIGGER GUARD   A loop of metal around the trigger to protect it from breakage and to help prevent accidental discharge of the gun.

TRUNNION   Studs projecting from the sides of a cannon and used as pivots to attach the weapon to its mount.

VENT   Same as touch hole.

VENT PICK   A pin used to clean powder residue from the vent.

WAD OR WADDING   A piece of paper, fabric, or leather to hold shot in the bore of a gun.

WHEEL LOCK   A forerunner of the snaphance. The cock, holding a piece of pyrite, is placed against a rough-edged steel wheel, which is spun by a spring. The spinning wheel, striking the pyrite, throws sparks into the pan.

WIPER   A device shaped like a double corkscrew that could be attached to the end of the ramrod of a muzzle loader. Cloth could be attached to it and used to clean a weapon's bore.

WORM   An alternate name for ball screw or wiper.

Bibliography

Andrist, Ralph K. 1967. *To the Pacific with Lewis and Clark.* New York: American Heritage Publishing Co.

Beeman, Robert D. 2000. Proceeding on to the Lewis & Clark Airgun." *Airgun Revue* 6:13–33.

Biddle, Nicholas. 1815. *Journals of the Lewis and Clark Expedition.*

Brown, Stuart E., Jr. 1968. *The Guns of Harper's Ferry.* Berryville, Va.: Virginia Book Co.

Carrick, Michael. "Meriwether Lewis's Air Gun." *We Proceeded On* 29, no. 4 (Nov. 2002): 13–19.

Clarke, Charles G. 1970. *The Men of the Lewis and Clark Expedition: A Biographical Roster of the Fifty-one Members and Composite Diary of Their Activities from All Known Sources.* Glendale, Calif.: Arthur H. Clark Co.

Cresswell, Mary Ann, ed. 1960. *Thoughts on the Kentucky Rifle in Its Golden Age.* York, Pa.: Trimmer Printing.

Fadala, Sam. 1982. *The Gun Digest Black Powder Loading Manual.* Iola, Wis.: Krause Publications.

Flayderman, Norm. 1998. *Flayderman's Guide to Antique American Firearms . . . and Their Values.* 9th ed. Iola, Wis.: Gun Digest Books (F & W Publications).

Furr, Clegg Donald. 1999. *American Swords & Makers' Marks: A Photographic Guide for Collectors.* Orange, Calif.: Paragon Agency Publishers.

Gibson, James R. *Otter Skins, Boston Ships and China Goods: The Maritime Fur Trade of the Northwest Coast, 1785–1841.* Seattle: University of Washington Press, 1999.

Gluckman, Arcadi. 1948. *United States Muskets, Rifles and Carbines.* Buffalo, N.Y.: Otto Ulbrich Co.

———. 1956. *United States Martial Pistols and Revolvers.* Mechanicsburg, Pa.: Stackpole Books.

Guthman, William. 1979. *Guns and Other Arms.* New York: Main Street Press.

Hartzler, Daniel D., and James B. Whisker. 1996. *The Southern Arsenal: Harper's Ferry.* New York: Old Bedford Village Press.

Held, Robert. 1973. *Arms and Armor Annual*, vol. 1. Northfield, Ill.: Digest Books.

Hicks, Maj. James E. 1957. *U.S. Firearms 1776–1956.* Beverly Hills, Calif.: Fadco Publishing.

———. 1979. *Notes on U.S. Ordnance*, vol. 1. Beverly Hills, Calif.: Fadco Publishing.

Hoyem, George A. 1981. *The History and Development of Small Arms Ammunition*, vol. 1: *Martial Long Arms: Flintlock through Rimfire.* Tacoma, Wash.: Armory Publications.

Hult, Ruby. 1960. *Guns of the Lewis and Clark Expedition.* Tacoma: Washington State Historical Society.

Jackson, Donald. 1962. *Letters of the Lewis and Clark Expedition with Related Documents 1783–1845.* Urbana: University of Illinois Press.

James, Charles: *Military Dictionary.* 1816.

Kauffman, Henry J. 1979. *The Pennsylvania-Kentucky Rifle.* Harrisburg, Pa: The Stackpole Company.

Lewis, Berkeley R. 1956. *Small Arms and Ammunition in the United State Service.* Smithsonian Miscellaneous Collections, vol. 129. Washington, D.C.: Smithsonian Institution.

Lindsey, Merrill. 1972. *The Kentucky Rifle.* New York: Arma Press.

Lister, C. B. 1950. *Simplified Small Arms Ballistics for the Sportsman and Soldier.* Handbook no. 2. Washington, D.C.: National Rifle Association.

MacKenzie, Alexander. 1927. *Voyages from Montreal on the St. Lawrence through the Continent of North America to the Frozen and Pacific Oceans, in the Years 1789 and 1793: With a Preliminary Account of the Rise, Progress, and Present State of the Fur Trade of That Country.* London, 1801. Toronto: Radisson Society of Canada (reprint).

Moller, George D. 1993. *American Military Shoulder Arms*, vol. 2: *From the 1790s to the End of the Flintlock Period.* Boulder: University Press of Colorado.

Moulton, Gary. 1985–2001. *The Journals of the Lewis and Clark Expedition.* 13 vols. Lincoln: University of Nebraska Press

National Rifle Association. 1959. *NRA Illustrated Indexed Questions and Answers Handbook.* Washington, D.C.: National Rifle Association.

Olsen, Kirk. May 1985. "A Lewis & Clark Rifle?" *American Rifleman.*

Olson, John. 1985. *Olson's Encyclopedia of Small Arms.* Piscataway, N.J.: Winchester Press.

Peterson, Harold L. 1964. *Encyclopedia of Firearms.* New York: E. P. Dutton.

———. 1965. *American Indian Tomahawks*. New York: Museum of the American Indian, Heye Foundation.

Reilly, Robert M. 1986. *United States Martial Flintlocks*. Lincoln, R.I.: Andrew Mowbray, Inc.. 1986.

Rodney, Thomas. *A Journey through the West: Thomas Rodney's 1803 Journal from Delaware to the Mississippi Territory*, ed. Dwight L. Smith and Ray Swick. Athens, Ohio: Ohio University Press, 1997.

Russell, Carl P. 1960. "The Guns of the Lewis and Clark Expedition." *North Dakota History* 27, no. 1: 25–34. Bismarck: North Dakota Historical Society.

———. 1962. *Guns of the Early Frontiers: A History of Firearms from Colonial Times through the Years of the Western Fur Trade*. Berkeley: University of California Press.

———. 1967. *Firearms, Traps, and Tools of the Mountain Men*. New York: Alfred Knopf.

Smith, Merritt Roe. 1997. *Harper's Ferry Armory and the New Technology*. Ithaca, N.Y.: Cornell University Press.

Smith, W. H. B. 1980. *Gas, Air and Spring Guns of the World*. Harrisburg, Pa.: Military Service Publishing Co.

Stewart, Henry, Jr. 1987. "The American Airgun School of 1800 (with Corollary Verification of the Lewis & Clark Air Rifle)." *Monthly Bugle* (February).

Whisker, James B. 1990. *Arms Makers of Pennsylvania*. Susquehana University. Cranbury, N.J.: Associated University Presses.

Wolff, Eldon. 1958. *Air Guns*. Milwaukee, Wis.: Milwaukee Public Museum (reprint).

Index

Page numbers in italic type indicate illustrations.
Page numbers followed by an "n" indicate footnotes.